CW01475610

Our Mother Mary's Warnings

At Civitavecchia, Akita, Garabandal and Fatima

William Timmerman, PhD

Our Mother Mary's Warnings
Civitavecchia, Akita, Garabandal and Fatima

August 2020

Pen Shop Publishing

San Antonio, Texas

William Timmerman, PhD

Table of Contents

Our Mother Mary's Warnings

At Civitavecchia, Akita, Garabandal and Fatima

Introduction

If you were to ask the Blessed Virgin Mary her favorite title and role, I believe she would say it is "Mother". She has been given many titles and roles throughout history. Some she has given to herself; others are connected to the locations of her apparitions such as Fatima, Garabandal, Akita and more recently Civitavecchia. Some titles are related to the messages she gives including Queen of Peace, Our Sorrowful Mother, Our Lady of Victory, Virgin Most Merciful. The Litany of Loreto contains at least fifty titles for Mary, but I still think she relishes those titles that begin with "Mother".

As a little boy, I went to Mother of God grade school right across the street from Mother of God Church less than two blocks from my home. It was a German church. Some older parishioners still called it "Mutter Gottes Kirche". I started serving at Mass when I was eight years old and still served as a twenty-two old adult until I moved away from Covington, Kentucky. I learned early on to say by heart the complete Rosary with all the Mysteries, the Hail Holy Queen and Memorare prayers and sang the favorite hymns to Mary in the school choir including the Ave Maria, Salve Regina, and the Magnificat. The Mass was said in Latin back then and we learned to sing Stabat Mater, an ancient Catholic hymn to Mary, which means "the sorrowful mother stood". The extended first line of the hymn is *"At the cross her station keeping, stood the mournful mother weeping, close to Jesus to the last."* She is at times a sorrowful and mournful mother.

After grade school I attended Covington Catholic High School taught by Marianist brothers and priests. I was a member of the Legion of Mary that required dedication to Christ through devotion to the Blessed Virgin Mary. Now you can see why I would be writing about her and singing the praises of the

Mother of God as early on I declared my undying devotion to this most beautiful and pure creation from God.

In 2020, Pope Francis added several more roles for the Blessed Virgin in the Litany of Loreto including the titles of Mother of Hope and Mother of Mercy. Catholics, among others, believe Jesus' mother is "Our Mother" too; we are her children. The principal Scriptural basis is found in the Gospel of John. At Calvary, Mary, Jesus' mother was by the foot of the Cross with John, Jesus' beloved disciple.

"When Jesus saw his mother, and the disciple whom he loved standing near, he said to his mother,

'Woman, behold your son.' Then he said to the disciple, 'Behold your mother'" (John 19: 26-27).

The Church believes and teaches that John is symbolic of all humanity. In other words, from the Cross Jesus gave His Mother to every human person for all time as our spiritual mother.

"So, your strength is failing you? Why don't you tell your mother about it?... Mother! Call her with a loud

3

voice. She is listening to you; she sees you in danger, perhaps, and she--your holy mother Mary--offers you, along with the grace of her son, the refuge of her arms, the tenderness of her embrace...and you will find yourself with added strength for the new battle."

- *Saint Josemaria Escriva*

Mary as Our Mother:

I present this background to explain why I believe the title and role Mary favors the most is "Mother". Although a mother of one when she walked this earth with her son Jesus, she is the mother of a great big family now. I see her as your mother, and she is my mother. She resides now in heaven and she comes to visit on many occasions. How many times have people claimed she has visited them? On his website "MiracleHunter. com, Michael O'Neil states, "Some scholars estimate the total number of apparition claims throughout history to be approximately 2,500 (with about 500 of those coming in the 20th century alone)." The International Marian Research Institute at the University of Dayton in Ohio reports there have been 386 cases of Marian apparitions from 1900 to 2011.

That published directory and O'Neil's site currently do not list the 1995 apparition of Mary at Civitavecchia, Italy that presents a thrilling story. It is the only apparition that I could find where a family consisting of a little daughter, her father and her mother were the principal visionaries. When addressed as visionaries, they said they would rather be called witnesses. The primary objective of this book is to spread awareness of this special event at Civitavecchia and the messages Mary gave to the family and for the world. I have discovered that most English-speaking people do not know about the Madonna of Civitavecchia. At the present time, I know of four books that have published the story in foreign languages, either Spanish or Italian. Two are by Father Flavio Ubodi, a Capuchin theologian, who played a prominent role in the story principally as the vice-president of the Diocesan Theological Commission. This commission examined phenomena which included a bleeding statue, testimonies from numerous eye witnesses, verifiable scientific test results and the reports of exterior celestial voices and apparitions reported by the family that experienced them. This author has drawn the most from published interviews with Father Ubodi, Archbishop Carlo Maria Vigano, former Apostalic Nuncio to the United States and Jessica and Fabio Gregori.

Apparitions are considered private revelations that Catholics are not required to believe even if they are approved by the local bishop or in a few cases by the Holy See. Private revelations cannot surpass, correct, improve, fulfill, complete, or perfect public revelation that was brought to completion with the death of Saint John the Apostle. Father Flavio said private revelations "are like a call to live what is already contained in Sacred Scripture, in Tradition, and they transport it into the urgency of the present time." Authentic private revelations often can motivate people to a greater commitment to avoiding sin, practicing a stronger prayer life, and living out a Christ-like life. Now for the awesome first story.

The Statues of Mary at Civitavecchia

The story begins on September 16, 1994 with a kind gesture by the local parish priest. Father Don Pablo Martin had returned from a pilgrimage to Medjugorje with an inexpensive souvenir statue of Mary called the Queen of Peace. He gave the small sixteen-inch white glazed statue to the Gregori family who belonged to his parish of Saint Agostino Church in Pantano, Italy to protect them from evil. Fabio Gregori was overjoyed with the gift and placed it in a small stone grotto he erected in their garden in the front yard.

On Thursday February 2, 1995, the Feast of the Presentation of Jesus in the Temple and the Purification of Mary, Fabio was putting his 18-month-old son David in the car, getting ready for the 4:30 pm Mass, when he heard Jessica, who was not yet six years old say, "Dad, Dad, the Madonna cries."

She said her father did not believe her and answered, "How does a chalk statue cry? It's 4:21 p.m., we're late for Mass." She then told him, "The Lady cries all the blood."

As soon as Fabio heard the word "blood", he ran toward Jessica, looked at the statue, checked Jessica's hands to see if she had hurt herself and was convinced the blood was from her. When he touched his finger to the red substance on the statue, he said, "A great blast of fire" surged through him (Sullivan, *The Miracle Detective,* pg. 46). He picked Jessica up and they rushed off to church. When they arrived, he told his wife Annamaria, who was already at church waiting for them all about it. Immediately after Mass, Fabio told Father Pablo what had happened and asked to go to confession believing that having touched the blood he had committed a sacrilege.

Annamaria would later remember a dream she had forgotten that depicted a painful event happening on the feast day of the Presentation of Jesus. The dream appeared to be intermixture of her own death with the sword that would pierce Mary's heart as prophesized by Simeon during the Presentation of Jesus in the Temple.

Over the next several days the phenomenon of the statue's bleeding eyes repeated itself a total of thirteen times in front of a crowd of witnesses including as many as ten different law enforcement officers Fabio had requested to protect the statue, a newspaper photographer and Father Don Pablo until February 6 when news of the mysterious phenomenon became a national news story. All of this took place in the little rural hamlet of Pantano of maybe 600-700 people, 3 to 4 miles away from the coastal town of Civitavecchia on the Tyrrhenian Sea, where ferries regularly leave for Sardinia. It is about 40 miles northwest of Rome.

The little bleeding statue of Mary became known as the Madonna of Civitavecchia. Carmela Dinardo, who runs Civitavecchia's foreign-language school claimed, "You couldn't move for cars, buses and people blocking the way to his residence. People had come from all over Italy. The Gregoris simply locked themselves inside the house." Overwhelmed by all the commotion, Fabio took the statue to Father Pablo for safekeeping. Fabio then locked the gates to his garden and put up a notice: "Please don't stop here. The Madonna is no longer here."

All the hullabaloo about the bleeding statue led Girolamo Grillo, the Bishop of Civitavecchia, who was skeptical about the whole affair, to confiscate the statue from Father Pablo after initially telling him to destroy it. He put it in a basket in a closet in his residence while people were wondering where the miraculous statue was. He had the police investigate the Gregori family and formed a Diocesan Theological Commission to investigate the phenomenon.

On March 15 after he had celebrated Mass, his sister asked him to bring the statue out of the closet. While his brother-in-law, nephew and two Romanian nuns also were present, he began reciting the "Hail, Holy Queen" prayer and when saying the line, "Turn then most gracious advocate, thine eyes of Mercy toward us," the statue cried blood while he held it in his hand. The shock was so great the bishop needed first aid from a cardiologist. His personal experience in front of witnesses erased the doubts in his mind at that time. He was no longer a skeptic.

On April 5th Bishop Grillo appeared on a national prime time newscast to tell about the marvelous occurrence. The newscast only served to impel the judicial system to further investigate the whole matter because there were already too many hoaxes of bleeding statues being perpetrated on the Italian public.

Giuseppe Lo Mastro, president of Codacons, Italy's largest consumer rights organization said, "We live in a world full of connivers, and in this country there are winds driven by the will for a miracle. What we are seeing is the development of a miracle industry, or miracle mass production."

With prompting from consumer rights protection organizations, the prosecutor's office took the little statue into custody and ordered numerous tests including CAT scans. It was determined that there were "no hidden devices" in the statue. Later, the statue was sequestered by the prosecutor's office back in the bishop's residence. A timeline of subsequent events included the following:

April 10, Pope John Paul II sent his personal representative to preside over a prayer vigil in the diocesan cathedral in reparation for the seizure of the statue and blessed a second identical statue from the Pope that was given to the Gregori family.

April 18, Bruno Forestieri, the Gregori family's attorney obtained the end of the sequestration.

June 11th, the statue was taken to Pope John Paul II at his request, and in secret, he looked upon the statue with great reverence, prayed before it and, placed a crown he had obtained on the Virgin's head. He later confirmed in writing this occurrence in a document dated October 8, 2000 that later was personally signed by him.

June 17, 1995, following a solemn and public procession, the statue of the Virgin Mary of Civitavecchia was enthroned in St. Agostino Church, the Gregori family's home parish in Pantano, and placed in a shrine dedicated to her for veneration (now protected by bulletproof glass), while the Theological Commission listened to the sworn testimony of many witnesses and the case of the miraculous bleeding statue would be studied at the Vatican.

In 1996, the Diocesan Theological Commission reached a decision that the event of the bleeding statue of the Madonna of Civitavecchia was judged "supernatural" and Bishop Grillo approved the decision. Bishop Grillo then forwarded the results to the Congregation for the Doctrine of the Faith, and on October 27, 1997, it announced the establishment of a Commission presided over by Cardinal Camillo Ruini. This Commission was dissolved without ever publishing a verdict, which means the confirmation of the Diocesan Commission's verdict stands.

Early on, a legal attack was directed at Fabio Gregori which went on for years accusing him of "abuse of public credulity" until October 16, 2000 when Judge Carmine Castalado proclaimed that there was "no trickery found" in the case of the mysterious happenings. When he learned of the decision, Fabio said, "I am happy that the case is closed but in conscience I must say I was always absolutely at peace."

That brings us to the existence of the second statue of the Virgin Mary of Civitavecchia. This statue was given to the Gregori family on April 10, 1995 by Cardinal Andrzej Maria Deskur and blessed by John Paul II. It is identical to the statue that bleeds but instead gives off fragrant, perfumed oil during some religious festivals or in front of people gathered in prayer. At times, the Virgin Mary herself has appeared and given messages to those present.

Anna María Turi, who wrote an Italian book about the Virgin of Civitavecchia, visited the Gregori's home on March 29, 2006. When Jessica said the statue had begun to cry, Anna looked at the statue and observed "the right eye, that it was swollen, therefore, noticeably different from the left (I was able to see, a few days later, how the two eyes regained the same dimension) emerged a white liquid that with the drops going down to the chin, formed a drop in suspension. The white, transparent, visible liquid, particularly between the arch of the eye and the beginning of the cheek, kept dripping and increasing the aqueous formation that formed below." She was allowed the opportunity to taste one of the tears. She said it had a "strong perfume of flowers… and was saltier than a common tear."

Anna's remarks remind me of what Jesus said, "You are the salt of the earth." One interpretation is that his disciples would be the salt, that as a preservative, could stop the moral decay of a sin infected world. I worked with a specialist in deliverance one time that sprinkled salt in a room he said to protect against evil spirits. Perhaps Mary's tears would be saltier than most human tears because Mary is the Devil's defeater as was first revealed in Genesis.

Archbishop Carlo Maria Vigano in the famous Lifesite interview, stated that he visited the Gregori family and met with Bishop Grillo in the 1990's. He saw the perfumed balm exuding from the base of the statue. The little stone shrine was surrounded by tall shrubs. Said Vigano, "The balm even exuded from the leaves of the shrubs, and a drop fell on my head." Later, he was able to hold the statue in his hands and has kept for himself a cotton wad soaked "in the miraculous balm" in a handkerchief along with the "small leaf from which a drop of the balm dripped onto my head."

Father Flavio Ubodi said that the balm is a sign of the protection of Mary and the graces of the Holy Spirit.

The two statues of Civitavecchia, as you can see, provide a fascinating story filled with drama, mystery, irony and most of all, a celestial atmosphere. Let us look at the many surprising connections and the interplay between the characters in this marvelous story.

The Many Surprises and the Notables Connected to the Story

Padre Pio now Saint Padre Pio played an important role in the story of the two statues of Civitavecchia. In the previous chapter we met Father Dom Pablo Martin, the parish priest who gave the little statue of Mary to the Gregori family.

Don Pablo had a strong devotion to Padre Pio. He claimed that, while in Medjugorje, Padre Pio helped him choose the statue he gave to the family. He understood from Padre Pio "the most beautiful event of his life" would result from selecting and buying that statue according to Randall Sullivan in this book *The Miracle Detective*. Padre Pio died in 1968. Don Pablo bought the statue in 1994. This would suggest that he received a supernatural message after Padre Pio died. The "most beautiful event" indeed did occur when the Marian statue's eyes started bleeding on February 2, 1995.

We already visited the second surprise. Bishop Grillo said, "I tore up the report (from Father Pablo) and threw it in the bin and told Don Pablo to destroy the statue immediately, so as to end all this trouble! I had no doubt it was a hoax. Naturally, I started hearing from angry parishioners condemning me for not believing in all this rubbish" (*Our Lady Weeps; Report on Civitavecchia*). Later, Bishop Grillo would turn from doubter to believer.

Which side are you on?

The state may have been dead set against the weeping statue, but the local mayor was all for it. Pietro Tidei, the 48-year-old mayor of Civitavecchia, a former communist and acknowledged agnostic, decided to hang a crucifix above his desk in city hall. He was exuberant when talking about the financial windfall the little statue will bring to the local economy that was suffering from a twenty-one percent unemployment rate. He talked about how long it will take the Vatican to decide if it is a real miracle or not and said, "We will not wait 20 years to bring in hot dogs and religious souvenirs," referring to the goings on at other apparition sites like Lourdes and Medjugorje.

More Surprises for Bishop Grillo

Earlier, the skeptical Bishop decided to have the statue scientifically analyzed. He requested his own doctor to test the "blood" congealed on the statue. He didn't anticipate the result: the tests indicated that the substance was hemoglobin. On February 10, 1995, the bishop personally takes the statue to Rome for analysis of the bloodstains and for x-rays of the structure by two different teams: the Institute of Legal Medicine of Gemelli Hospital led by Professor Angelo Fiori, and Rome's leading forensic medical examiner and DNA expert, Giancarlo Umani-Ronchi, director of the Institute for Forensic Medicine at the University of Rome. It will remain there until February 28 when it is returned to the bishop. The statue was placed in a closet in the room of a Romanian nun, Tereza Duma, who serves at the residence of the bishop.

The series of x-rays of the statue itself confirmed that it was solid, with no sign of having been altered. The blood test results provided the biggest surprise. It was human blood all right, but the hematic fluid of the tears corresponded to male gender; however, with strong female connotations. Why would that be? Bishop Grillo responded, "That actually increased my doubts. Obviously, it had to be a hoax. The blood of Our Lady ought to have been female, no?"

Fabio's answer appeared to make total sense. It is the blood of Jesus that he "shed for all the children who turn away from her Immaculate Heart, to give you salvation" (May 17, 1995). When asked about the bloody tears in an interview, Father Ubodi said, "Our Lady begged us: "Don't make me cry My Son's blood anymore"! Fabio added, "In Civitavecchia, a Mother showed us Her terrible suffering because the blood of Her Son flows in vain. There is nothing more to add: the event itself in Civitavecchia is a message" (Canioto, 2015 interview).

Surprising Connections to Famous People:

In addition to St. John Paul II's confirmed belief in the statue of tears of blood, other famous spiritual leaders pronounced their belief in the miraculous statue. Mother Teresa affirmed her believe in the miraculous event and was very devoted to Our Lady of Civitavecchia. At one point, she asked the Gregori family to meet her in Rome to talk about their experiences as she was too ill to travel to Pantano.

Other spiritual leaders expressed their belief including Chiara Lubich, founder of the Focolare, a world-wide Catholic movement devoted to the ideal of unity between all nations, religions and races. Luigi Giussani expressed his belief in the supernatural phenomena at Civitavecchia. He was the founder of the Communion and Liberation movement, now in ninety countries, which emphasizes "education in the Catholic faith that doesn't end at a certain age, but lasts a lifetime because it is always being renewed and deepened."

The late Father Gabriele Amorth, renowned chief exorcist of Rome, strongly believed in the apparitions, and reportedly visited the Gregori family frequently, asking them to pray for him when he was at the end of his life. He had begged the bishop in the beginning to have faith in the miraculous events because one of his spiritual daughters foretold a statuette of Our Lady would weep tears of blood at the gates of Rome six months before it actually happened.

In April 2005, when Pope Benedict XVI greeted Bishop Girolamo Grillo at the end of the Italian Episcopal Conference, he said that the Madonna "will do great things".

In the next chapter, we will learn that in 1996 Jessica Gregori met with Sister Lucia dos Santos, Fatima's last seer, and that they shared with one another in private what they knew about the mysterious Third Secret given by Our Lady of Fatima. Father Ubodi said, "…from what I know from Jessica, they compared the messages … and they matched perfectly."

The Messages from the Madonna of Civitavecchia

Fabio Gregori stated that between 1995 and 1996 the family received 93 messages, "two of which were secrets to our bishop and a third to the Pope, in a cycle of public appearances to my daughter and me."

The national and international news reports and many of the published secular articles place the entire focus on the bleeding statue and little to nothing about the underlying messages. They dwell on how the red streams of blood got on the statue instead of why they were there. All the secular news and investigative stories stop short of the spiritual meaning of the spectacular event that began on February 2, 1995.

Beginning on February 6, 1995, Fabio heard an external voice talking to him. In time, the entire family gradually experienced external voices sometimes from God the Father, Jesus, or Mary as spiritual manifestations. Then, beginning in July

1995, a series of apparitions of Jesus, Mary and angels began to happen, presenting numerous messages that ended for a while on May 17, 1996. Fabio shared one particular apparition.

On July 16, 1995 at 6:30 p.m., during Mass, he said, "Our Lady stood right above Father Pablo, her feet immersed in a white cloud, her arms open with her hands facing the ground." When Father Pablo was about to consecrate the host, she remained silent in adoration, Fabio believed, to emphasize that her Son Jesus is truly present and alive in the Eucharist.

In the Gregori family garden on August 27, 1995, the Blessed Virgin said, "My children, the darkness of Satan is now obscuring the Church of God. Prepare to live what I revealed to my little daughters at Fatima…after the painful years of Satan's darkness, the years of the triumph of my Immaculate Heart are now imminent." Here we have the first clear connections between the state of the Church, Mary's Immaculate Heart, and Fatima.

On May 17, 1996 Jessica said in an interview, "The main message is that they want to destroy the family. And then the apostacy in the Church and the risk of a third world war."

The Blessed Virgin appeared again on December 23, 2018. The message included a great warning. *"Your Nation is in grave danger. In Rome darkness is descending more and more on the Rock that my Son Jesus left you on which to build up, educate and spiritually raise his children. Bishops, your task is to continue the growth of God's Church, since you are God's heirs."*

"Consecrate yourselves all to me, to my heart, and I will protect your Nation under my mantle now full of graces. Listen to me, please, I beg you! I am your heavenly mother, I beg you: do not make me weep again seeing so many of my children die for your faults by not accepting me and allowing Satan to act."

In another message at Civitavecchia the Blessed Virgin said, "Satan is trying to destroy the Church of God "by means of many priests…"

Simeon's prophecy to Mary when Jesus was presented in the Temple to God came true with Christ's Passion and Mary's symbiotic passion. With his crucifixion, Mary, his mother must have felt "a sword will pierce your own soul too" (Luke 2: 35).

Mary and Jesus are obviously genetically linked. Her blood is his blood. The blood poured out by Jesus would come forth again in Mary's tears on the statue. Recall that the scientists determined that the blood was from a male with strong female aspects, a fact which would support that the little statue cried the blood of Jesus through her feminine eyes. The probing frank question the reoccurrence of Jesus' bleeding raises is: Did Jesus shed his blood in vain for us? Look at the world today. Haven't we seriously strayed from the path leading to the salvation of our souls? Have we betrayed the love in the blood he poured out for us?

Mary is a loving mother. As a mother, she cares deeply about our physical and spiritual welfare. She keeps repeating the same messages each time she appears. This book now focuses on four specific occasions when she presented detailed warnings about what the future holds for us if we do not change our sinful ways. Her apparitions particularly at Fatima, Garabandal, Akita and Civitavecchia are examined individually and collectively for a clear understanding of her messages to us. You will find that the dominant messages are repeated at each location but one of the messages will be more prominent depending on the location of her apparitions.

Mary's three dominant messages at all four apparition sites are:

1. Families are being attacked by Satan

2. The shepherds of the Church are leading its people astray

3. Something monumentally earth-shaking is going to happen if we do not change our sinful ways

With every threat of danger to our God-given souls, Mary tells how we can protect and save ourselves physically, mentally, and spiritually. Because we are easily distracted by the things of the world, she must be very stern with us to get our attention. We need to take to heart her dire messages. Just as a mother warns her child to not touch a hot stove, she is warning us and reminding us of the fires of hell. Her messages are intended to be a serious wake-up call. If we don't change our way of living, we are playing with moral suicide and the potential consequence of losing our own souls.

Satan's Threat to Families

"Through her maternal help, may every Christian family be a "little church" in which the mystery of Christ is relived" (John Paul II, November 22, 1981). Pope John Paul II's former secretary Monsignor Emery Kabongo said when visiting Civitavecchia,

"The future of the Church and the world depends on the unity of the family."

Mary's message is singularly special to Civitavecchia. On July 16, 1995 at 6.00 am, Our Lady revealed: "Satan wants to destroy families". Father Ubodi noted, "The message of Civitavecchia is characterized above all by the family – that is, the destruction of the family, of the primordial cell of society" (Daily Compass). He went on to cite the numerous threats to the family including divorce, abortion, same-sex marriages, among others.

Mary and Jesus selected the Gregori family for a good reason. They were a "little church" unto themselves. Fabio, an electrician by trade, was considered a devout and faith-filled family man by his parish priest. His wife Annamaria, as noted earlier, was a recipient of revelations in the form of dreams including the specific one about the feast day of the Presentation of Jesus in the Temple. Jessica received many messages. When she was about 15 years-old, she too told a reporter that the family had received 93 messages. Father Ubodi noted, "Our Lady communicated her messages orally in the apparitions, which were immediately transcribed by Fabio or Jessica" and then passed on to Bishop Grillo.

Like every family, the Gregori have two great families to model themselves after. First, the Holy Trinity is the divine family of three persons of "undivided unity" and mutual love shared with one another. The Blessed Virgin said in Civitavecchia, "The Lord has clothed me with His Light and the Holy Spirit with His Power. My task is to take all my children away from Satan and bring them back to the perfect glorification of the Most Holy Trinity."

Mary, Joseph, and Jesus comprise a second model human family we can emulate. The mutual love they shared and sacrifices they made for one another shine forth as a wonderful example of what is possible when a family follows God's will and lives out his plan for them. Fabio said, "Heaven wanted to reiterate that the family is the heart of human society and the Church. Through this sign he asks all families to make an effort to follow the example of the Family of Jesus."

When asked how all the excitement has affected him, Fabio said, "My life as a husband and father of a family has not changed; my Christian being has changed profoundly."

On December 23, 2018, the Virgin Mary appeared to Fabio and Annamaria during Holy Mass. Here are portions from her message to them as a family:

Always be bearers of love, prudent in knowing how to discern Satan's traps. Always be free from all human compromise and always listen to God who speaks in the intimacy of your Heart. Always be salt of the earth, light of the world, growing in the virtue of our Holy Family of Nazareth so that every human family may draw in our witness the path of faith, hope, and love. And the Most Holy Trinity will refound the true and new family of God as established by Him.

It is interesting to note, that "Queen of Families" was added to the Litany of the Blessed Virgin on

31

December 31, 1995 by Pope John Paul II eleven months after the Statue of Mary first bled and later was brought to him at the Vatican. Bishop Grillo claimed that the pope also secretly visited the Gregori family and the statue on several occasions.

One of Satan's major goals is to attack and destroy families.

Apostasy in the Church

As we will see later, the message from Mary given to the four visionaries at Garabandal was an early warning of what was to come for the Church. Some believe that the part in the message about cardinals, bishops and priests leading people astray more than fifty years ago is the possible reason why the local bishop of the diocese has not approved the Garabandal apparitions. Back then, the growing scourge of clergy child sexual abuse and the devious movement to over-modernize the Church remained secret from the public.

Both Father Ubodi and Archbishop Vigano agree that Fatima and Civitavecchia are jointly connected in proclaiming the apostacy within the current Church. Ubodi spoke about a denial of the Tradition, dogmas, the truths contained in the Creed that is going on. Vigano referred to Mary's message to the Gregori Family: "My children, the darkness of Satan is now obscuring the whole world and it is also obscuring the Church of God. Prepare to live what I had revealed to my little daughters of Fatima."

Vigano recalled a famous statement from Cardinal Pacelli in 1933 who later became Pope Pius XII: *"I am concerned about the messages of the Blessed Virgin to little Lucia of Fatima. This insistence on Mary's part on the dangers threatening the Church is a divine warning against suicide through the alteration of the Faith, in her Liturgy, in her theology and in her soul... I feel around me the innovators who want to dismantle the Sacred Chapel, destroy the universal flame of the Church, reject her ornaments, and inflict regret on her for her historical past."*

Vigano contends that the real message from the Third Secret of Fatima is about the apostasy within the Church. Nearly fifty years ago in June 1972, Pope

Paul VI wrote: "… We would say that, through some mysterious crack—no, it's not mysterious; through some crack, the smoke of Satan has entered the Church of God. There is doubt, uncertainty, problems, unrest, dissatisfaction, confrontation. The Church is no longer trusted…"

We now prepare ourselves for Satan's third goal that Mary shared with the Gregori family and with Sister Agnes Sasagawa at Akita as we will see later.

The Wake-Up Calls from Mary Keep Coming

Mary is a loving mother. She wants her children to have happy and peace-filled lives but that will happen only if they follow what God asks of them. The way is clear. We are to know, love and serve God. And, we are called to love and treat others as we would expect for our self. But that is not what is happening. We, like the leaders of the Church, have gone seriously astray from God's plan and desires for us. Our Lady of Fatima prophesized what would happen if people do not repent for their sins against God. Jesus gave up his life as a sacrifice for our salvation, but too many people have rejected him and gone on with their sinful ways of living. What happened back then? World War II came.

She asked the pope to specifically consecrate Russia to her Immaculate Heart. Scholars claim that has never been done as the message was spelled out. Consequently, Russia spread its evil influence and remains a dangerous treat to world peace. We are reminded that Jessica Gregori stated that the last part of Mary's three-part messages was "the risk of a third world war".

Our Lady told the Gregori family, *"Satan knows that his time is running out because my Son Jesus is about to intervene. I beg you, help me; do not let my Son intervene, because I, your Mother, want to save many souls and bring them to my Son and not leave them to Satan. Pray that God our Father will grant me some more time, because this is the last period granted to me by God. My mantle is now open to all of you, full of graces, to place you all close to my Immaculate Heart. It is about to close; then my Son will deliver his divine justice..."* (July 30, 1995). Jesus is merciful toward those who repent of their sins and dispenses justice in a corrupt world. Jesus is just and he is also merciful.

Riccardo Caniato in 2015 asked Fabio Gregori (Catholic Studies No. 652 June 2015) What kind of war are we talking about?

Fabio's response: The threat of a nuclear conflict between the West and the East, the third world war.

He later said, "Our Lady asked me and my family to live and witness the message she gave here. And in her apparitions, she referred to Fatima: "I chose Fatima for the beginning of the twentieth century", she said, "Civitavecchia on her end".

Our Lady of Fatima

On May 13, 1917 Lucia, Francisco, and Jacinta took their flock of sheep to graze, just outside the town of Fatima in Portugal. They were ages 10, 9 and 7 at the time. While the sheep were content and the children were playing, there was a sudden flash of lightening. The children looked up, bewildered into the sky. They started to gather the sheep thinking a storm was brewing in the distance. Although the day was pleasant so far and there was no other sign of bad weather, then there was a second flash that caused alarm.

A few meters away stood a Lady of dazzling light. Their eyes were unable to comprehend the lady's brilliance and beauty.

The children smelled roses.

"Where are you from?" Lucia managed to ask.

"I am from Heaven", the lady replied.

"What do you want of us?" asked Lucia.

"I came to ask you to come here on the thirteenth day of each month for six months at the same time."

The lady asked them to say the Rosary daily and inserting, "O My Jesus, forgive us our sins, save us from the fires of hell and lead all souls to heaven, especially those who are in most need of Thy mercy" between the mysteries, then she rose in a cloud of light and glided away into the sky. Lucia warned her two cousins to say nothing about what happened because nobody would believe them, but Jacinta told her parents about the apparition. They had trouble believing her. Lucia's mother accused her of lying and punished her when she refused to deny her story. Other children mocked them when they heard about it.

On June 13, 1917, Blessed Mary appeared the second time again reminding the children to pray the Rosary every day and for Lucia to learn to read and write. Lucia was told she would live longer than the other two children to spread the messages of Mary throughout the world. She told Lucia that God wants to "establish devotion to my Immaculate

Heart in the world." Whoever embraces it is promised salvation. She said that Francisco and Jacinta would be in heaven very soon, but Francisco will have to pray many Rosaries.

Only Lucia speaks to the Mary. Jacinta can see and hear her while Francisco can only hear her.

On July 13, 1917 during her third apparition, Mary revealed three secrets involving prophetic visions. The first secret was a vision of what Hell looks like "where the souls of poor sinners go" and Mary told them that to save future souls God wants the world to become devoted to her Immaculate Heart. "If what I say to you is done, many souls will be saved and there will be peace."

The second secret was the prediction that World War I would end, but she warned if people didn't stop offending God, a worse one will break out during the pontificate of Pius Xl. She said, "When you see a night illumined by an unknown light, know that it is the great sign that God gives you, that He is going to punish the world for its crimes by means of war, hunger, persecution of the Church and of the Holy Father." To prevent this, she asked for the dedication specifically of Russia to her Immaculate Heart, and the Communion of Reparation on five First Saturdays.

"If my requests are heeded, Russia will be converted, and there will be peace; if not, she will spread her errors throughout the world, causing wars and persecutions of the Church. The good will be martyred; the Holy Father will have much to suffer; various nations will be annihilated. In the end, my Immaculate Heart will triumph. The Holy Father will consecrate Russia to me, and she shall be converted, and a period of peace will be granted to the world to prevent the damage that Russia would do to humanity by embracing communism."

Pope Pius XI did not consecrate Russia to the Immaculate Heart of Mary. The October Revolution in Russia led to it becoming the first Communist country and its "errors" have spread throughout the world.

On January 25-26, 1938, the night illuminated by an unknown light did come to pass as Mary had prophesized and the world-wide press covered it. The headline on the New York Times was "Aurora Borealis Startles Europe". Other sources reported that it was visible as far south as Australia and as far west as California. People claimed that it looked like a big forest fire.

The Third Secret was not revealed for over twenty-five years. Lucia was pressured by Bishop da Silvato finally to write it down in early 1944. In the vision, the children saw a bishop dressed in white (who they thought to be the pope) walking towards a mountain with other priests and religious figures. Their journey would take them through a town that is in ruins and the pope prays for the souls of the corpses he passes along the way. As they reach the top of a mountain, the pope kneels before a cross and he and the others are killed by soldiers.

Unlike the previous visions, there is no explanation from Mary and this has fueled the debate about why it took so long for the Third Secret to be revealed and what the complete and true message contained.

Pope John Paul II believed this vision referred to his own assassination attempt on May 13, 1981. We will see what other Church authorities have to say about the Third Secret later and its connections to Jessica and Our Lady of Civitavecchia and to other Marian apparitions.

The fourth apparition was expected on the 13th of August 1917, but the three children were prevented from going. There was a climate of political anti-clericalism at that time, and they were held by authorities, who threatened them with punishment if they did not renounce the apparitions. Later, they were released and saw Mary on August 19th. She urged them to continue to pray the Rosary and told them to pray, pray very much, and make sacrifices for sinners. "Many are going to hell because no one is praying and making sacrifices for them."

More than 30,000 people were present for the fifth apparition on September 13, 1917 and were praying the Rosary before the three children arrived. The people wanted to see Mary but she was seen only by the children who then described the apparition to them. Lucia asked Mary, "What do you want from me?" The Blessed Lady replied: "Continue to pray the Rosary in order to obtain the end of the war. In October, Our Lord will come, as well as our Lady of Sorrows and Our Lady of Carmel, Saint Joseph will appear with the Child Jesus to bless the world. In October I will perform a miracle so that all may believe."

On October 13, 1917 the children were surrounded by a crowd of 70,000 people blanketed by torrential rain that started the night before and was continuing when the Blessed Mary appeared and revealed her identity: "I am the Lady of the Rosary, I desire here a chapel in my honor to be built, that people continue to recite the Rosary every day. The war is going to end, and the soldiers will soon return to their homes. Do not offend the Lord our God anymore, because He is already so much offended." Then the miracle she promised happened.

The Miracle of the Sun

Mary opened her hands and launched a ray of light in the direction of the sun; the rain stopped suddenly and there appeared an exceptionally bright sun. Everything suddenly dried up. The sun began to turn, projecting colorful bands of light. Then the sun appeared as if it was spinning out from the sky and towards the crowd, as people fell to their knees and begged for mercy. Meanwhile, as promised, the three children saw the Blessed Lady dressed in white with a blue cape, along with St. Joseph with the Child Jesus blessing the world. Then after this vision they saw the Lord bless the world, standing next to Our Lady of Sorrows. After this vision vanished, they saw Our Lady once more, this time resembling Our Lady of Mount Carmel.

An investigation of the Miracle of the Sun provided concurring testimony from secular reporters, government officials, and other skeptics that attended the extraordinary event leading to the Church's determination that it was a "supernatural" event. On October 13, 1930, Bishop Jose de Silva declared the miracle "worthy of belief".

As a side note, it is easy to see all the curious interconnections related to the thirteenth of the month between the Fatima apparitions, the assassination attempt on Pope John Paul II, Bishop Silva's declaration and also the thirteen times the statue of the Madonna of Civitavecchia bled in the presence of the Gregori family. Some Catholic broadcasters have noted the repeated phenomenon of thirteen. Now add the month of October and the thirteen day. October 13 is the date of Pope Leo XIII's vision of Jesus and Satan, the date of the final apparition of Our Lady of Fatima and it is the date of one of the main apparitions of Our Lady of Akita! However, the writer has wondered whether the fourteenth time when the statue bled in the hands of Bishop Grillo could not be connected to the fourteen Stations of the Cross. As Jesus was bleeding profusely and painfully returning to his feet after falling the first time, his mother Mary sees her tortured, bloody Son as the Fourth Station of the

Cross. She must have remembered Simeon's prophecy as she felt a sword piercing her heart.

The Third Secret Controversy

Pope John XXIII read the 'Third Secret" in August 1959 but decided not to publicize it. Pope Paul VI made the same decision in March 1965. As noted, when Pope John Paul II read it, he believed the Third Secret was connected to the assassination attempt on his life on May 13, 1981. During the Pope's visit to Fatima, Cardinal Angelo Sodano explained the "third secret" in general terms, linking the "bishop dressed in white" in a fight with atheistic systems to the assassination attempt against the Holy Father in May 1981.

When faced with serious questions about what the real third secret is, Cardinal Bertone, in a press conference in April 2000, declared "The Third Secret has nothing to do with the apostasy linked to the Council, the Novus Ordo (of the Mass) and the conciliar Popes, as the integrists have claimed for decades." Cardinal Ratzinger, and later when he was Benedict XVI, has appeared to waffle about what the third secret really contains. In the beginning he appeared to follow the party line that the vision pertained primarily to the assassination attempt. Cardinal Ratzinger writes: "Those who expected exciting apocalyptic revelations about the end of the world, or the future course of history are bound to be disappointed. Fatima does not satisfy our curiosity in this way, just as Christian faith in general cannot be reduced to an object of mere curiosity." However, on May 13, 2010 (there's the 13th again) when he went as pontiff to Fatima again, he stated, "One would be deluding oneself if one thought that the prophetic mission of Fatima is over."

Cardinal Mario Luigi Ciappi, Father Flavio Ubodi and Archbishop Vigano have stated that the true contents of the Third Secret have been hidden by the Church from the public for reasons of self-incrimination. Father Joaquin Alonso, the official Fatima archivist, in his book *The Secret of Fatima: Fact and Legend*, believes that the Third Secret concerns the crisis of Faith within the Church, and the "internal struggles in the very bosom of the Church and of grave pastoral negligence by the upper hierarchy."

Father Ubodi asserted: "Cardinal Ciappi, who had read the Third Secret of Fatima, specified that the Virgin had said that the apostasy would be initiated from the top of the Church." Archbishop Vigano reminds us that Pope John XXIII on February 8, 1960, stated that the Church "does not wish to take on the responsibility of guaranteeing the truthfulness of the words that the three shepherd children said the Virgin Mary spoke to them." Vigano alleges that the Vatican early on in the 1960's began "a cover-up operation" to bury the true contents of the Third Secret.

Here are two primary questions at play in the controversy. In 1957, Bishop José da Silva prepared to fulfill the Vatican's request to have Lucia's letter about the Third Secret sent to it in the still-sealed envelope. Before it was sent, Auxiliary Bishop John Venancio held it up to a strong light, and saw that it contained a single, folded sheet of paper with about 25 lines of handwriting on it and margins of 3/4 centimeter on either side. The Third Secret that was released by the Vatican is four pages. The second big question is why did it take until 2000 for the secret to be released when Lucia stated it would make sense to people ("it will be clearer then") as early as 1960?

As noted earlier, Archbishop Vigano and Father Ubodi say the messages from Civitavecchia and Fatima are the same. In fact, they affirm that Jessica Gregori met with Sister Lucia to discuss the messages in 1996 in private. Father Ubodi said, from "What I know from Jessica, they compared the messages of the Blessed Mother and they matched perfectly. There is a remarkably close relationship between Fatima and Civitavecchia." Sister Lucia has since died, and Jessica has promised to keep the contents Mary gave her secret.

Mary had told Jessica at Civitavecchia, "Prepare yourselves to live through everything I revealed to my little daughters at Fatima." Our Lady of Fatima prophesied about a coming war and that Russia will be a threat to the world. What was so secret that her revelation of what the vision meant is not available? Father Ubodi reminds us of the possible answer. "Cardinal Ciappi, who had read the Third Secret, specified that the Virgin had said that the apostasy would begin from the top. In my opinion, this is the great prophecy."

Recall the revelation at Garabandal that "cardinals, bishops and priests" received back in the 1960's will lead followers astray.

We return to Pope Benedict XVI who was a cardinal at the time.

In the "third secret," Sister Lucia writes about the vision of an angel with a flaming sword. That image, Cardinal Ratzinger notes, is a common one from the Book of Revelation, and it represents "the threat of judgment which looms over the world." During the 20th century, when warfare threatened millions of people with instant annihilation, that threat of judgment became particularly immediate, he observes.

Some people with investigative minds believe the message released by the Vatican is not the "real secret". They believe the true message of the Third Secret was revealed by Mary in her apparition at Akita, Japan, in 1973, that "the work of the devil will infiltrate the Church ... cardinals opposing cardinals, bishops against bishops." Supporters of this message said the Fatima message and Akita message are linked.

The former Philippine ambassador to the Vatican, Howard Dee said in a 1998 interview with Inside the Vatican magazine: "Bishop Ito (Bishop of Niigata where the diocese of Akita is located) was certain Akita, where he was an eyewitness to the miraculous events and determined they were of supernatural origin, was an extension of Fatima. Dee added, "Cardinal Ratzinger personally confirmed to me that these two messages, of Fatima and Akita, are essentially the same."

Our Lady of Akita

The apparitions of the Blessed Virgin Mary in Akita, Japan to Sr. Agnes Sasagawa began on June 12, 1973 after she was led by an angel to the chapel where she saw brilliant mysterious rays emanate suddenly from the tabernacle. The same thing happened on each of the next two days that preceded apparitions by the Virgin Mary. On January 4, 1975, the statue of Mary in the chapel began to weep like the two statues in Civitavecchia. It cried three times on that first day.

The weeping statue drew so much attention that its crying was broadcast on national television throughout Japan on December 8, 1979. The final time the statue cried was on the feast of Our Lady of Sorrows that occurred on September 15, 1981. Recall that Mary presented herself as Our Lady of Sorrows during the final apparition at Fatima. It is reported that the Our Lady of Akita statue had wept for a total of 101 times.

Tears, perspiration, and blood samples taken from the statue were scientifically tested by people who did not know where the samples came from. The results proved to be of human origin and the blood types were determined. The blood was found to be Type B, the sweat Type AB, and the tears Type AB. It is fascinating because samples from the Shroud of Turin and the Sudarium of Oviedo that allegedly wrapped the body of Jesus were Type AB.

At one point, Sister Agnes developed a very painful bloody wound in her right hand in the shape of a cross that was designated a stigmata that followed after the appearance of blood on one of the hands of the statue that some said formed something like a cross.

The statue sometimes bled simultaneously with Sister Agnes. She had the stigmata on her hand for about one month from June 28 to July 27 and the statue of Mary in the chapel bled for a total of about two months.

When she was feeling great pain caused by the stigmata in her hand the angel said, "The wounds of Mary are much deeper and more sorrowful than yours" as we recall Simeon's prophecy that a sword would pierce Mary's soul as she witnessed her Son's tortuous suffering ending in his Crucifixion.

The angel taught Sister Agnes the same prayer that Mary taught the children at Fatima. "Oh, my Jesus, forgive us our sins, save us from the fires of hell, and lead all souls to heaven, especially those in most need of your mercy. Amen."

Our Lady of Fatima warned of future disasters "If people do not repent and better themselves." At Akita, Mary presented this dire message to Sister Agnes on October 13, 1973:

"If people do not repent and better themselves the Father will inflict a terrible punishment on all humanity. It will be a punishment greater than the deluge (the flood involving the prophet Noah that the Bible describes), such as has never been seen before. Fire will fall from the sky and will wipe out

*nearly all of humanity – the good and the bad,
sparing neither priests nor faithful. The survivors
will find themselves so desolate that they will envy
the dead. The devil will rage especially against
souls consecrated to God. The thought of the loss of
so many souls is the cause of my sadness. If sins
increase in number and gravity, there will no longer
be pardon for them."*

As recently as October 6, 2019, Sister Agnes was
visited by an angel and given this message. "Put on
ashes and pray a repentant Rosary every day. You
must become like a child and make sacrifices every
day." The message sounds remarkably familiar. It is
basically the same message Mary gave the children
at Fatima with the two qualifications added of
"ashes" and "repentant". Why would that be? There
are two interesting connections. That day was the
exact same day Pope Francis welcomed the
Pachamama into the Vatican Gardens considered by
many to be a pagan goodness on the very day the
Amazon Synod started. The second connection is
also intriguing. The reading at Mass two days later

came from Jonah 3:1-10. Jonah tells the people of Nineveh that God is greatly displeased with what is going on in Nineveh and the city is in danger of being overthrown. "When the news reached the king of Nineveh, he rose from his throne, laid aside his robe, covered himself with sackcloth, and sat in ashes." Then he proclaimed that all the people should fast, put on sackcloth and cry out to God for mercy. "When God saw by their actions how they turned from their evil ways, he repented of the evil he had threatened to do to them; he did not carry it out." (Mystic Post, November 3, 2019). Rumor has it that sometime later Sister Agnes confided to a "Sister M" that "I feel the time is near" suggesting some type of punishment is imminent but not the end of the world.

The Apparitions at Garabandal

San Sebastián de Garabandal is a tiny village of about three-hundred people living in Northwest Spain. On June 18, 1961, four girls, between eleven and twelve-years-of-age named Conchita, Jacinta, Mari Loli, and Mari Cruz suddenly encountered an apparition of an angel shortly after they had stolen some apples from the headmaster's tree. The angel did not speak then or numerous times later until he announced that the Virgin Mary would appear to them on July 2, 1961. Later, he identified as Michael the Archangel. Four years after he first appeared, he would give a frightening message to the children on behalf of the Virgin Mary.

On July 2, 1961 they received the first visit from Mary as Our Lady of Mount Carmel. The early visits took place in a grove made up of nine tall majestic pine trees. After the first encounter, there were more than two thousand visits from the Virgin Mary and Michael the Archangel between 1961 to 1965 that took place at various places in and around the village.

When the young girls were in ecstasy during the apparitions, they did not show any signs of pain from multiple pin pricks. At times they would levitate or crash down on their knees on jagged rocks without any indications of pain or bleeding. They would run so fast to where they were summoned interiorly (inner signal calls) by Mary to meet her that people could not keep up with them. Sometimes they would walk backwards extremely fast while their heads were tilted back looking skyward without ever falling. They did not blink when burning matches or bright lights were shined in their faces. When not in ecstasy, they appeared as normal children for their age. They were playful, mannerly, devout, very used to working and shy and humble around adults.

At times, Mary would appear holding the baby Jesus. They claimed Mary kissed many religious objects passed by people in the crowd that the girls would not know who to return them to. Mary would interiorly guide them back to the rightful owners. Mary even gave them her crown to try on. The interaction between the four girls and Mary was playful at times as she would help guide the seeker during "hide and seek" games. Like a mother, she taught them to pray slowly and fervently. At other times, she would correct them if they were chewing gum, for example, and would remind them to be obedient to their parents and the Church. On one occasion the girls in unison added "and **our** mother" after the "holy Mary mother of God" part of the Hail Mary prayer. She said she liked it, but they should not add it to the prayer until the Church approved it.

A most remarkable event took place when Conchita visibly received the sacred host on her tongue from Michael the Archangel that can be seen on a photograph available on the Internet. She had made the request to Michael to show that they really were receiving the Holy Eucharist previously unseen by the on-watchers.

We now turn to the messages given by the Virgin Mary and by Michael the Archangel to the four children and for the world.

October 18, 1961 from Mary

"We must make many sacrifices, perform much penance, and visit the Blessed Sacrament frequently. But first, we must lead good lives. If we do not, a chastisement will befall us. The cup is already filling up, if we do not change, a very great chastisement will come upon us."

June 18, 1965 Mary's dire message delivered by Michael the Archangel

"As my message of October 18th has not been complied with and has not been made known to the world, I am advising you that this is the last one. Before, the cup was filling up. Now it is flowing over. **Many cardinals, many bishops, and many priests are on the road to perdition and are taking many souls with them. Less and less importance is being given to the Eucharist.** You should turn the wrath of God away from yourselves by your efforts. If you ask His forgiveness with sincere hearts, He will pardon you. I, your mother, through the intercession of Saint Michael the Archangel, ask you to amend your lives. You are now receiving the last warnings. I love you very much and do not want your condemnation. Pray to us with sincerity and we will grant your requests. You should make more sacrifices. Think about the passion of Jesus."

When Jacinta was asked what message from Mary struck her the most during all the apparitions, she said, "The Blessed Virgin seemed to prefer the most…was the subject of priests." In a 1973 interview with Conchita, Dr. Jerome Dominguez asked, "What do you think about the statement that cardinals, bishops and priests are on the road to perdition? Conchita answered,
"I think every day the Virgin appeared she mentioned priests and that we should pray for them. We never understood why. For us priests were like saints because we never had many come to our village. It was considered a privilege whenever one came. Regarding bishops and cardinals, we thought it very strange, but we would repeat it the way she said it."

The part of the message from Mary about "cardinals, bishops and many priests" totally shocked the local bishop and hierarchy of the Roman Catholic Church.

65

At that time, it seemed to come out of nowhere and made no sense to them. People at that time could not believe it was a true prophecy because they could not foresee the future. What was starting to happen back then has become a full-blown reality as the Catholic Church today is being rocked by scandal and threats against Catholic teaching and Tradition that includes cardinals, bishops, and priests. Many supporters of the Garabandal apparitions believe that is the underlying reason why the local bishop or the Vatican has not approved the apparitions. Did Conchita get the message right?

On October 13, 1973, the anniversary of Our Lady's last apparition at Fatima and the Miracle of the Sun, Mary gave her third message to St. Agnes Sasagawa at her convent in Akita, Japan. Mary began her third message with this statement: "The work of the devil will infiltrate even into the Church in such a way that one will see cardinals opposing cardinals, bishops against bishops…"

Who in 1973 would see part of it unfolding today, 45 years later? Her warning was most dire.

Let's now look at the three major events prophesized by the Virgin Mary: The Warning, then a Miracle, and if the Warning and the Miracle do not turn people back to God, the Chastisement will follow. Many people have hazarded guesses of when the Warning and the Miracle will take place. Some thought it would have happened by now. Some of the girls were given specific details about the Miracle, for example, that it will happen at "8:30 pm on a Thursday in the month of April" but not the year. Mari Lori stated she was the only one who knew the exact date of the Great Miracle but did not reveal it before she died in 2009. A key variable in any prediction model is that, based on the statements from the girls, the Warning will come when the world is at its worst whatever that means and whenever that will be.

The Miracle according to Conchita:

- It will be the greatest miracle that Jesus will have performed for the world. There won't be the slightest doubt that it comes from God and that it is for the good of mankind.

- The sign that will remain forever at the "pines" is something we will be able to photograph, televise and see, but not touch. It will be evident that it is not a thing of this world but from God.

Conchita said she will give notice to the world eight days in advance of its occurrence. The Warning will precede the Miracle within a twelve-month period. Conchita is now over seventy years old and it is presumed that she will give the notice before she dies. Recall that the Warning is to come first as a purifying event in preparation for the Miracle.

The third event called the dreaded Chastisement is conditional. It will depend upon how humans respond to the two earlier events. If we don't shape up, then we will feel something like the "night of the screams" the four children experienced when the Virgin Mary shared with them what the Chastisement would be like. Many people will die and those who survive will wish they were dead. The Warning will feel much like the burning flames of Purgatory without the physical pain but with severe spiritual turmoil; the Chastisement will feel like being in Hell itself.

Warnings from Heaven to Other People in the Past

Though the time may not be yet, it cannot be far distant

Saintly people down through the ages have spoken of specific warnings coming from heaven.

In the 1500s, St. Edmond Campion stated, "I pronounce a great day, not where, in any temporal potentate should minister, but where in, the Terrible Judge, should **reveal all men's consciences** and try every man of each kind of religion. This is the day of change, this is the Great Day which I threatened, comfortable to the well-being, and terrible to all heretics."

Blessed Anna Maria Taigi in the nineteen century experienced visions of the future. In one of those visons she described a future warning from God that would lead many people to repent of their sinfulness. "A great purification will come upon the world preceded by an Illumination of Conscience in which everyone will see themselves as God sees them."

In the twentieth century, St. Faustina described a vision she experienced when she stood alone before the Lord. "Suddenly I saw the complete condition of my soul as God sees it. I could clearly see all that is displeasing to God. I did not know that **even the smallest transgressions**, will have to be accounted for." At another time Jesus told her, "Write this: before I come as the Just Judge, I come as the King of Mercy. Before the day of justice arrives, this sign in the sky will be given to mankind. All light in the heavens will be extinguished, and there will be great darkness over the whole earth. Then the sign of the Cross will be seen in the sky, and from the holes where the hands and the feet of the Savior were nailed will come forth a brilliant light, which will illuminate the Earth for a period of time. This will take place shortly before the last day." (xxxviii), Diary entry, August 2, 1934.

Maria Esperanza, a modern-day Catholic mystic from Venezuela who died in 2004, was told by the

Virgin Mary that "A great day of light!" is coming. In response Maria said, "We must awaken to the love of God. In the coming years, a new light from heaven will illuminate hearts, but before it does there will be hardship." She added, "The consciences of this beloved people must be violently shaken so that they may "put their house in order" and offer to Jesus the just reparation for the daily infidelities that are committed on the part of sinners. . . it is the hour of decision for mankind."

You can find many others who believe in a forthcoming Warning and the Illumination of Conscience in Christine Watkins' popular book, *The Warning: Testimonies and Prophecies of the Illumination of Conscience*.

The Virgin Mary's Warning at Garabandal

In summary, the Warning will enable every man, woman, and child all over the world to see the state of their own soul through an illumination of conscience as God sees their soul. It will be a private revelation between each person and God. It will be like the "particular" judgment that each person goes through immediately after dying, when the person is shown all the events and actions in one's life, as in a detailed biographical life review experience. The advantage of the Warning is the person will be presented the opportunity to change their life for the better that is not possible once you die.

For years following the apparitions at Garabandal, the four recipients of Mary's Warning revealed specific details in their responses during various interviews. Some of those specific details are shared below. The reader can review the sources of the complete interview responses in the Bibliography. The main source is the Garabandal International Magazine, October-December, 2004.

CONCHITA

September 14, 1965

Q. Will the Warning be a visible thing or an interior thing or both?
A. The Warning is a thing that comes directly from God and will be visible throughout the entire world, in whatever place anyone might be.

October, 1968

Q. We have heard that some say the Warning may be a natural phenomenon but will be used by God to speak to mankind. Is this true?
A. The Warning is something supernatural and will not be explained by science. It will be seen and felt.

1973

Q. What will occur on the day of the Warning?
A. The most important thing about that day is that

everyone in the whole world will see a sign, a grace, or a punishment within themselves — in other words a Warning. They will find themselves all alone in the world no matter where they are at the time, alone with their conscience right before God. They will then see all their sins and what their sins have caused.

February 1977

Q. *Would you repeat for us what you know about the Warning?*
A. It is a phenomenon which will be seen and felt in all the world and everywhere; I have always given as an example that of two stars that collide. This phenomenon will not cause physical damage, but it will horrify us because at that very moment we will see our souls and the harm we have done. It will be as though we were in agony, but we will not die by its effects but perhaps we will die of fright or shock to see ourselves.

MARI-LOLI

September 29, 1978

Q. *Since you are the one who knows the most*

about the Warning will you tell us if this event is to take place before the Miracle promised through Conchita Gonzales?

A. ... Everyone will experience it wherever they may be, regardless of their condition or their knowledge of God... It will be an interior personal experience. It will look as if the world has come to a standstill, .. .no one will be aware of that as they will be totally absorbed in their own experience.

October 19, 1982

Q. Do you remember what the Blessed Mother said about the communist tribulation that is to precede the Warning?

A. It would look like the communists would have taken over the whole world and it would be very hard to practice the religion, for priests to say Mass or for people to open the doors of the churches.

JACINTA

February 1977

Q. Can you tell us what the Warning will be like?

A. The Warning is something that is first seen in the air everywhere in the world and immediately is transmitted into the interior of our souls. It will last for a short time, but it will seem an awfully long time because of its effect within us. It will be for the good of our souls, to see in ourselves our conscience, the good and the bad that we've done. Then we'll feel a great love toward our heavenly parents and ask forgiveness for all our offences.

The Warning is for everybody because God wants our salvation. The Warning is for us to draw closer to Him and to increase our faith. Therefore, one should prepare for that day, but not awaiting it with fear because God doesn't send things for the sake of fear but rather with justice and love and He does it for the good of all His children that they might enjoy eternal happiness and not be lost.

Connie Hoebich, in a 1974 article titled "The Warning" said, "I believe that the warning will go easier for us to the extent that we prepare for it now through penance and the overall fulfillment of the message of Garabandal." This statement is totally in line with this book's major premise that we should prepare ourselves by analyzing our sinful behaviors in order to aid us in a serious sustained effort to not sin again and to lead a virtuous life. Jesus made it truly clear to the woman who committed adultery. "Go and sin no more." He is telling her to say "no" to the sin that dwells in her and stop the desire from being conceived; stop the temptation from becoming sin. The same applies to us. Assume a prayerful attitude and petition God for those "close moments" that can lead to spiritual introspection and self-revelation. Ask Jesus, Mary and the angels and saints to help you face the sin in your life and cry out in sorrow to God for his mercy and forgiveness.

It would seem wise to enact a serious plan to make mid-course corrections right now, not tomorrow for no one knows when the Warning will come. The four young seers at Garabandal said the state of the world was very "bad" back then. That was fifty-five years ago. When we look at the world today, the signs of the times appear much worse. Communist China among other countries is actively persecuting Christians. To my knowledge Russia has never been consecrated to the Immaculate Heart of Mary as Our Lady of Fatima specified and looms as an ever-present danger to world peace. Violence, hatred, racism, abortion, mass murders, suicides, drug abuse, sexual abuse abound in America and around the world. Furthermore, the Catholic Church presently is besieged by sexual scandal and inferences of apostasy through the abandonment of formerly held beliefs that incriminates even the highest level of officials within the Church.

The Virgin Mary's message of June 18, 1965 at Garabandal, stating "Many cardinals, many bishops, and many priests are on the road to perdition and are taking many souls with them" seems to have foretold what has happened. Nobody could understand or believe back more than some fifty-five years ago that a sensational prediction like that could possibly be true including Bishop Gallo of the diocese of Santander in the Ecclesiastical province of Oviedo in Spain. In a 1992 interview he was asked, "Were the Garabandal Messages found to be theologically correct and in accordance with the teachings of the Church?

His answer: "I think yes. Theologically correct, yes.

But one of the details bothers me like the one: 'Many bishops and cardinals are walking the path of perdition' it seems to me to be a bit severe.'" Some experts believe that the same exact prediction was embedded in the Third Secret of Fatima and that the Vatican has done its best to conceal that part of the Fatima secret from the public.

Five years later after the revelation that many cardinals, bishops, and priests will lead souls to hell, Pope Paul VI in 1970 stated,

"Many of the faithful feel troubled in their faith due to an accumulation of ambiguities, uncertainties and doubts that touch upon essential matters of their faith. Such are the Trinitarian and Christological Dogmas, the mystery of the Eucharist and the Real Presence, the Church as Institute of Salvation, the Priestly Ministry in the midst of God's People, the importance of prayer and the Sacraments, moral demands related, for example, to the indissolubility of Matrimony or the respect of human life" (Quinque Iam Anni, December 8, 1970).

If "many of the faithful" felt troubled back then, how many more have become appalled by the betrayal of the "essential matters of their faith?" A recent survey cited by Auxiliary Bishop Robert Barron claimed, "For every person who joins the Church, 6.4 members are leaving the Church" and most are leaving at young ages, primarily before age 23. The median age of those who leave is 13 (Carol Zimmermann, Catholic News Service, June 12, 2019).

One can surmise that as the people on earth become more and more wicked and deny the loving God, the Warning is becoming more imminent. The four visionaries have attempted to describe what the Warning will be like. It will be some type of supernatural astronomical phenomenon that will draw the attention of everybody in the world. It will be so terrifying that people will stop in their tracks, fall on their knees, and cry out for God's mercy. They will feel an overwhelming sense of anguish in their inner being that they would prefer to die rather than undergo the experience. They will feel like the earth is standing still, frozen in time, in total silence. They will confront the ugliness of all the sin in their lives and will be racked with agony and a sense of panic. Some will be so shocked by what they see, they will have a heart attack and die. But the four visionaries claim that the event will not involve physical harm rather it will center full throttle on one's conscience.

There are obvious connections between Fatima and Akita as there are with Civitavecchia and Garabandal.

We need only to focus on the prophetic visions related to the sky. The four seers of Garabandal spoke of a future spectacular astrological event that will announce the Warning. Our Lady of Fatima warned of a forthcoming spectacle in the sky that the news media considered a rare manifestation of Aurora Borealis, which signaled the oncoming World War II. The war ended with an explosion of Atomic bombs that blew up in the sky over two cities in Japan killing approximately 200,000 people. And, as she foretold at Fatima, the sun on

October 13, 1917 performed an unbelievable dazzling display for ten minutes that frightened many people, some fearing it was the end of the world.

"Chastisement" was the scariest message Mary gave at Garabandal and sounds like what Mary described to Sister Agnes at Akita: "…fire will fall from the sky and will wipe out nearly all of humanity…" Recall Fabio Gregori's earlier remark about the threat of "a nuclear war between the east and the west."

In the Old Testament, God promised Noah that He would never again destroy the earth by a flood. However, some verses in the Bible suggest that the world will be destroyed someday by fire citing, for example, 2 Peter 3:10: "But the day of the Lord will come like a thief, and then the heavens will pass away with a roar, and the heavenly bodies will be burned up and dissolved, and the earth and the works that are done on it will be exposed." That would suggest something like what a nuclear war would cause.

We can only hope and pray that the "Chastisement" Mary described to the four children at Garabandal and the similar sounding threat of world-wide disaster revealed to Sister Agnes by Mary do not come to pass. Neither premonition is connected to The Final Judgment or end of the world, however, it will seem like it to the people who witness the Chastisement.

If the prophecies from Garabandal are true, it would seem wise that steps be taken to prepare for the Warning. We first can turn to Mary for her help.

Mary As Our Protector

"In trial or difficulty, I have recourse to Mother Mary, whose glance alone is enough to dissipate every fear."- *Saint Therese of Lisieux*

Mary's messages at each of the four apparition sites can strike terror in people's hearts. The Warning from Garabandal can be so fearsome Conchita thought that some people may die from fright seeing how sick their souls are. The Chastisement Mary shared with the four girls led them to a "night of screams".

The three children at Fatima were given a vision of hell that scared them so much they devoted the rest of their lives to constant praying and offering up sacrifices to save souls from going to hell. They were made aware of a forthcoming devastating World War II if people did not heed her warning to turn their lives toward to God. The Third Secret's vision revealed many martyrs and the leader of the church likely the Holy Father (*"a Bishop dressed in white"*) being killed after he had walked through a city in partial ruins while he prayed for the souls of the corpses he met on his way;

Sister Agnes at Akita was told by Mary that the world will be rocked by a great punishment. "As I told you, if men do not repent and better themselves, the Father will inflict a terrible punishment on all humanity. It will be a punishment greater than the deluge, such as one will never have seen before. Fire will fall from the sky and will wipe out a great part of humanity, the good as well as the bad, sparing neither priests nor faithful. The survivors will find themselves so desolate that they will envy the dead."

More recently at Civitavecchia, the Gregori family learned from Mary that Italy their country was in danger of destruction. Mary also prophesized that there would be a nuclear World War III between the east and the west if the world doesn't change. All these dire messages and scary prophecies were placed in the hands of humble recipients for them to alert the world that if we do not become a more God-loving people terrible things will happen to our world. But Mary made it truly clear that as a mother she is all about protecting her children.

> "Listen, my son, to your father's instruction
> and do not forsake your mother's teaching"-
> Proverbs 1:8

We are challenged to listen to her. She told us how to protect ourselves and the world from a terrible punishment. Pray the Rosary. Offer up sacrifices. Partake of and adore the Holy Eucharist. Personal conversion by a daily examination of conscience and frequent confession. Love God, love "your neighbors". Consecrate your family and yourself to Mary's Immaculate Heart.

On July 30, 1995 Our Lady at Civitavecchia said: "Satan is taking control of humanity, and now he is trying to destroy God's Church through many priests..." Earlier she stated, "My children, the darkness of Satan is now obscuring the whole world and it is also obscuring the Church of God. Prepare to live what I had revealed to my little daughters of Fatima" thereby linking the two apparition sites.

The cosmic struggle between the Mary and the Devil was foretold in Genesis 3:15 that in the end the Woman would crush the head of Satan. It is found again in the Book of Revelation chapter 12 where we are told of the struggle between the Woman Clothed with the Sun and the Great Red Dragon. Mary has made it clear to the visionaries and to us that she can protect us against Satan. Exorcists proclaim that Satan and his demons absolutely hate the Rosary. It is Satan's nemesis. For evil spirits it serves as a deadly sword that runs them away. The Rosary is an ultimate weapon of protection that Mary offers us to ward off sinful temptation that evil spirits use to try to corrupt us.

Immediately after the revelation of the Third Secret to Jessica at Civitavecchia, came the joyful promise from Mary: "Dear children, after the painful years of Satan's darkness, now the years of the triumph of my Immaculate Heart are imminent." As she has promised the three Fatima children and us, "In the end my Immaculate Heart will triumph."

Mary our mother will protect us if we give our self to her for safe keeping. As Mother Teresa told us to say, "Mary be a mother to me now" and forever. Amen.

Mary Is a Jewish Mother

"May the mother of Jesus and our mother, always smile on your spirit, obtaining for it, from her most holy son, every heavenly blessing."- *Saint Padre Pio*

At Garbandal, the visionaries estimated Mary appeared to look about seventeen years of age and "tallish". St. Michael the Archangel appeared to be about nine years old to them. This suggests that Mary and St. Michael can assume any bodily image they want. Why would St. Michael assume an image of a nine-year-old? The logical reason is that he did not want to scare the four girls away.

Most Marian statues present a white-skinned European type figure with fine features, thin hands, and fingers. The visionaries in the book *The Apparition of Garabandal* described Mary with a rather long face and with a "very dainty nose". In real life, Mary was a Middle Eastern Jew born in Nazareth. It is doubtful that her skin color was very white, and she was tallish. Sources say most women at Mary's time averaged about 5 feet tall. Her skin probably was more olive-brown, with brown eyes and dark hair. The Divine Mercy image of Jesus is clearly of a European white-skinned male. It seems, when Mary, Jesus or St. Michael appear in an apparition they can present themselves in a form that suits the situation based on the age, location, and culture of the visionaries.

We can have our own ideas of what Mary as a Jewish mother would look like and be like. Before we look at Mary from that perspective, let's compare what the visionaries tell us about what she was like as a person. At all four places featured in the book, she comes across most often in a sorrowful, deadly serious manner. She is a teacher but uses most of the time to warn them of serious dangers looming in the future and what they can do to alert others and protect themselves. At Garabandal, we see a different side of Mary. She seems more relaxed and shows interest in their lives and the homey stories from the four girls. She engages in "hide and seek" with them when she guides them to return the items she has blessed to their rightful owners that they could not have remembered without her help. Mary comes across as a more complete mother at Garabandal.

Conchita's wrote in her diary, "We told her that everyone was behind with the hay-making, and still had the grass piled waiting to be spread dry. And she laughed at the things we told her."

We hear another side of Mary from Fabio Gregori in his interview with Riccardo Caniato.

How is Our Lady?
She's beautiful. And it's mom, with a mom's heart.

What strikes you most about your attitude towards her and your family?
The discretion, the delicacy of mind, which even makes her apologize, in the act of appearing, for the time she takes away from others: "Fabio", she said just like that, "I apologize for the time I take away from your family".

What were Jewish mothers like at Jesus' time? Tzvi

Freeman shared his ideas in "Eight Great Things About Jewish Mothers. Really" (Chabad.org). Here are some of their characteristics. They value their children more than they value adults. They want their children to be knowledgeable about life and know all about God and grow up to "be somebodies" like doctors and rabbis. As Freeman puts it, "With a Jewish Mother, you'll come out an educated mentsch."

Jewish mothers provide more hugs and kisses than other mothers and they have no trouble talking to God and negotiating with him. As he notes, who do you think God is going to listen to first? Jewish mothers are assertive. They don't mess around.

Don't these descriptions of a Jewish mother sound like the Virgin Mary and her relationship first with Jesus as a young boy growing up and now that they are together in heaven? He was a rabbi on earth, and she continues to assert herself with Jesus the divine rabbi in heaven and intervene on our behalf to hold back the punishment we certainly deserve as a sinful people. Thank God she was and is a Jewish mother. The Jewish mother would detest ever being accused of neglect.

As St Alphonsus de Liguori quoted Novarinus, "If Mary, unmasked, is thus prompt to succor the needy, how much more so will she be to succor those who invoke her and ask her for help."

Mary Intercedes for Us

"Mary places herself between her Son and mankind in the reality of their wants, needs and suffering." John Paul II

An intercessor is one who takes the place of another or pleads another's case. Non-Catholics can have a problem accepting Mary as an intercessor before God. They claim, why not go directly to God? "I pray to Jesus; I don't need anyone between me and Jesus." Why is she even in the middle?

However, throughout Judeo-Christian history, religious leaders have served as intercessors with God. Moses is a great example. God was truly angry with the Israelites for worshiping a golden calf. Moses pleaded with God not to destroy them. God relented and did not destroy the Israelites.

Abraham negotiated with God to try to spare Sodom and Gomorrah from total destruction.

Unfortunately, in the end, there were not even ten righteous people in Sodom and Gomorrah for God to spare the cities. And recall Jonah's success intervening with God to save Nineveh from being overthrown.

Jesus is the ultimate intercessor with God the Father. He offered his body and blood as the total sacrifice for our salvation. The Blessed Virgin Mary is the Queen of Heaven. She was Jesus' mother on earth. As his mother, she demonstrated her influence with Jesus at the wedding feast at Cana. Mary noticed that the wine had run out and feeling pity for the humiliated family she turned to Jesus and said:

"They have no more wine."

He said, "O woman, what have you to do with me? My hour has not yet come" (John 2:4). Jesus' initial response shows that he didn't want to do what Mary asked.

His mother said to the servants, "Do whatever he tells you." (John 2:3-5). He does what his mother says and performs his first recorded miracle turning the water into wine revealing his glory as the Son of God. Mary's caring motherhood had influence on Jesus then; she has influence with him now in heaven.

Mary made it clear at Akita that she has influence with Jesus. On October 13, 1973 she told Sister Agnes, "Pray very much the prayers of the Rosary. I alone am able still to save you from the calamities which approach. Those who place their confidence in me will be saved." She can save us by interceding on our behalf with Jesus to hold off the punishment that the world deserves.

At Garabandal Mary said, "I, your mother, through the intercession of Saint Michael the Archangel, ask you to amend your lives. You are now receiving the last warnings. I love you very much and do not want your condemnation. Pray to us with sincerity and we will grant your requests." Mary as Jesus' mother is a powerful intercessor with her son, the most powerful one there is. She is our mother too and we have the advantage of asking her to intercede on our behalf with Jesus. In these critical times, it is good to remember what Sister Lucia said about our mother Mary. In the 1957 interview with Father Augustin Fuentes, Sister Lucia said God has given us "the last means of salvation, His Holy Mother."

What We Can Do to Prepare for the Warning

"If people, who are called by my name, will humble themselves and pray and seek my face and turn from their wicked ways, then I will hear from heaven, and I will forgive their sin and will heal their land" (2 Chronicles 7:14).

Here is what Jessica Gregori said we must do:

- Much prayer before Jesus in the Eucharist.
- Go to Holy Mass every day.
- Confession at least once a week, on the day of the Lord.
- Recite the Holy Rosary.
- Consecrate oneself to the Immaculate Heart of Mary.

Civitavecchia 01/01/2005

In faith,

Jessica Gregori

Fabio shared this: "Our Lady asks us to dedicate ourselves to her and to live our lives in the presence of God. To approach the Sacraments frequently, in particular the Eucharist and the Holy Confession; to meditate on the Rosary. But he explained that if we learn to turn our thoughts to God at all times of the day, then work, rest, friendships, everything becomes prayer."

Our Lady of Fatima said we are to:

Amend our lives

Pray the Rosary every day

Offer sacrifices for the conversion of sinners and the salvation of souls

Make the Five First Saturdays Communion of Reparation

Mari Loli, the young seer at Garabandal summed up Mary's message that we are "to do much penance, make sacrifices, visit the Blessed Sacrament every day that we are able to, and to pray the Holy Rosary."

The Power of the Rosary:

Our Lady of Fatima asked the three children to say the Rosary daily and to insert, "O My Jesus, forgive us our sins, save us from the fires of hell and lead us into heaven by your mercy" between each group of the mysteries. At Akita, Sister Agnes Sasagawa said her guardian angel taught her the same short prayer insert to Jesus in the Rosary. Each time Mary appeared at Fatima she reminded the children to pray the Rosary every day. More than 30,000 people were present for the fifth apparition on September 13, 1917 and were praying the Rosary before the three children arrived. At the final apparition on October 13, she declared "I am the Lady of the Rosary, I desire here a chapel in my honor to be built, that people continue to recite the Rosary every day."

At Garabandal on July 31, 1961, Loli said, "Sometimes Our Lady said the Hail Mary with us, but only to teach us to say it right." On August 18, the visionaries said she emphasized the need "to think" about the words and phrases that were being recited and what they meant.

Father Ubodi pointed out that at both Fatima and Civitavecchia that the recitation of the Rosary is the best weapon to defeat Satan, a weapon that drives away every danger to the soul and other dangers as well. Archbishop Vigano too, emphasized that praying the Holy Rosary daily is, "a powerful weapon to defeat Satan."

When Our Lady of Akita appeared to Sister Agnes, she said, "The only arms which will remain for you will be the Rosary (against a chastisement) and the Sign left by My Son. Each day recite the prayers of the Rosary. With the Rosary, pray for the Pope, the bishops and priests."

Sister Lucia told Father Fuentes in a 1957 interview:

"Look, Father, the Most Holy Virgin in these last times in which we live has given a new efficacy to the recitation of the Holy Rosary. She has given this efficacy to such an extent that there is no problem, no matter how difficult it is, whether temporal or above all, spiritual, in the personal life of each one of us, of our families, of the families of the world, or of the religious communities, or even of the life of peoples and nations that cannot be solved by the Rosary."

If you are unfamiliar with the Rosary, may I suggest Edward Sri's *Praying the Rosary Like Never Before: Encounter the Wonder of Heaven and Earth.* Father Patrick Peyton, who was known as "The Rosary Priest" and founder of the "Family Rosary Crusade", said, "The family that prays together stays together".

The Power of Sacrifices:

I should not be praying for my suffering to be removed, but for the strength to bear it and offer it up to God.

During the fourth apparition at Fatima on August 19, the Blessed Virgin urged the children to continue to pray the rosary and told them to pray, pray very much and make sacrifices for sinners. She said, "Many souls go to Hell because there are none to sacrifice themselves and to pray for them." In 1916 an angel appeared to the three children at Fatima three different times before Our Lady of Fatima first appeared on May 13 a year later. He said he was the

Angel of Peace and told the children to "Offer prayers and sacrifices constantly to the Most High . . . Make of everything you can a sacrifice, and offer it to God as an act of reparation for the sins by which He is offended, and in supplication for the conversion of sinners . . . Above all, accept and bear with submission the sufferings which the Lord will send you."

The vision of hell given the children at Fatima during the third apparition seemed to affect little Jacinta the most. To rescue sinners from hell, she was in the forefront leading Lucia and Francisco in voluntary mortifications. The children gave up their lunches to children poorer than them, sometimes even to their sheep. They refrained from drinking water in the heat of the day and wore a rough knotted rope around their waists that rubbed against their bare skin. At one point, Mary told them to not wear the rope in bed at night.

The Blessed Virgin stressed the importance of sacrifices to the children at Garabandal. On October 18, 1961 she said to the four girls, "We must make many sacrifices, perform much penance, and visit the Blessed Sacrament frequently. But first, we must lead good lives."

Suffering can be very painful but much good can come from it. Consider childbirth that can be one of the most painful experiences a person can experience.

"When a woman is giving birth, she has sorrow because her hour has come, but when she has delivered the baby, she no longer remembers the anguish, for joy that a human being has been born into the world" (John 16:21).

Women are willing to endure the agony of childbirth because it results in a blessed event, a baby.

It has taken me many years to accept the spiritual ramifications of suffering as an effective means of coping with the many challenges of daily life. It has radically changed my perspective about what really matters in life. Henri Fredric Ariel claimed, "You desire to know the art of living, my friend? It is contained in one phrase: Make use of suffering."

If you want to know more about sacrifices, I suggest *Offering It Up for Souls and the World* that I wrote a few years ago.

Consecration to Mary's Immaculate Heart:

The Our Lady of Fatima repeatedly called for the consecration of Russia to her Immaculate Heart to stop the damage Russia was doing to humanity by spreading the evil influence of communism. The Consecration of Russia to the Immaculate Heart of Mary required the specific act of the Pope along with all the Catholic bishops of the world at one time as specified in 1917 by Our Lady of Fátima. Finally, on March 25, 1984, Pope John Paul II declared, "Before you, Mother of Christ, before your Immaculate Heart, I today, together with the whole Church, unite myself with our Redeemer in this his consecration for the world and for people, which only in his divine Heart has the power to obtain pardon and to secure reparation." Critics claim the Pope did not specifically state "Russia" in the consecration, quite possibly for political reasons, thereby not fulfilling Our Lady of Fatima's detailed order.

People may consecrate themselves to any saintly person such as St. Joseph that has a direct and sacred relationship with God. Father Donald Calloway recently published a book titled *Consecration to St. Joseph: The Wonders of Our Spiritual Father.* In Bishop Athanasius Schneider's book, *Christus Vincit: Christ's Triumph over the Darkness of the Age*, he shares that around age sixteen, he consecrated himself to his guardian angel.

Father Ubodi stated, "The messages of both Fatima and at Civitavecchia speak of consecration, not entrustment; there is a profound difference. Entrustment is more superficial, while consecration is much more powerful because it involves the entire person, family, Church, or nation that makes it. It is like saying, "I am yours; I hand over to you my entire being, so that you may deliver it to the Father." Our Lady of Fatima told the shepherd children that Russia could be stopped from spreading it errors if it was consecrated to her Immaculate Heart. She promised, "In the end, my Immaculate Heart will triumph." At Civitavecchia, Mary told Jessica Gregori and Bishop

Grillo that the Country of Italy was in great danger and needed to be entrusted to Mary's Immaculate Heart. On December 8, 1996, Bishop Grillo, through a solemn public celebration, consecrated the diocese and the City of Civitavecchia to the Immaculate Heart of Mary. Mary invites us to consecrate ourselves and our families under the mantle of her Immaculate Heart to gain her guidance and protection. In the appendices you will find prayers of consecration to the Immaculate Heart of Mary.

The Eucharist-the source and summit of the Catholic faith:

Earlier in the book, Fabio shared how during Mary's apparition at Mass she demonstrated absolute reverence as Father Pablo consecrated the sacred host to emphasize that her Son Jesus is truly present and alive in the Eucharist. Mary Loli said Mary wants us to visit the Blessed Sacrament every day. This includes not only receiving Holy Communion but giving time for adoration of the Blessed Sacrament.

Father Ubodi was asked, "Did Mary at Civitavecchia also say what are the weapons to defeat Satan and triumph with Her?"

He responded, "Love, prayers, humility, the Rosary and the true conversion of hearts to God, through consecration to Her Immaculate Heart and to the Heart of Her Son. As well as the Eucharist, Eucharistic Adoration and the Sacraments."

Archbishop Vigano said in the Lifesite interview, "The messages strongly call people to return to the sacramental life, they speak of the need to be nourished with Eucharistic Communion, daily if possible; to go to Confession regularly "on Sundays" (a discreet emphasis on the important of receiving Communion in the state of grace); they invite people to Eucharistic adoration. There is a strong call to personal prayer, to placing oneself in the Presence of Jesus in the Eucharist for at least a quarter of an hour a day…"

During the COVID-19 pandemic, Catholics who cannot attend a live Mass are able to receive spiritual communion through a specific prayer request that can be found in the appendices.

Why Our Mother Desires Our Consecration to Her Immaculate Heart

Above all else, guard your heart,

for everything you do flows from it. Proverbs

4:23

In Old Testament times, people did not regard the human heart as simply an anatomical organ. To them, it was the central core of a human being. When Mary asks us to unite our hearts with her Immaculate Heart, she is offering a spiritual heart linkage that includes mind, emotions, and conscience. She desires us to "give" our whole being to her care. The images of Mary's Immaculate Heart and Jesus' Sacred Heart show their hearts placed outside of their bodies. I believe the images symbolize the fact that their love for us is infinite and cannot be bound by any barrier whatsoever. At Civitavecchia in September of 1995, she promised *"My Immaculate Heart will transform your sufferings into joys which you accept with true love, for these are trials which the Lord Jesus allows.* " (Vigano)

The reverse image on the Miraculous Medal helps explain the unity of their two hearts.

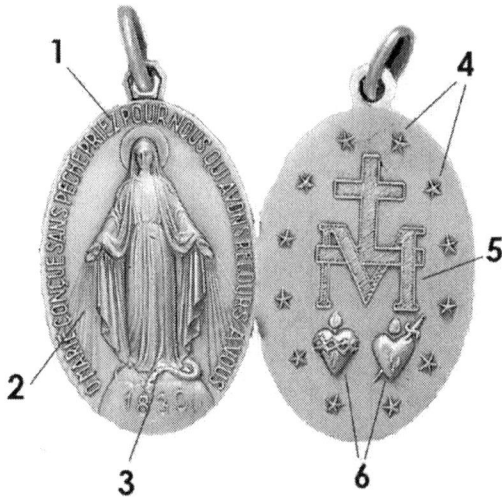

6 points to two hearts. Jesus' Sacred Heart is on the left. It is crowned with thorns. Mary's heart is on the right. Her Immaculate Heart has a sword pierced through it as prophesized by Simeon at the Presentation of Jesus at the Temple. The fire shooting up from each heart symbolizes the purity

and intensity of love between Mary and Jesus that is shared with us if we are open to it.

1. THE PRAYER: From Latin to English, "O Mary! conceived without sin, pray for us who have recourse to thee!". These words surrounded Blessed Mary in the vision to St Catherine in 1830.

2. THE RAYS: projecting out from Our Lady's hands symbolize the graces shed upon those who ask for them.

3. THE GLOBE: Mary is standing on the globe crushing a serpent representing Satan below her virginal feet. The image symbolizes her Assumption into Heaven as the Queen of Heaven and Earth.

4. THE STARS: The twelve stars on the back of the medal symbolize the Twelve Apostles who formed the original Church and the verse from the Book of Revelation, "a great sign appeared in heaven, a woman clothed with the sun, and the moon under her feet, and on

her head a crown of 12 stars" (Revelation 12:1).

5. THE M WITH THE CROSS: The M stands for Mary, the Mediatrix who presents our prayers to her Son to seek His graces. The Cross and Bar surmounting Mary's name symbolizes Christ suffering on the cross and redemption. It also reminds of her presence at the foot of the cross at her Son's death.

The "1830" commemorates the year when the Blessed Virgin appeared to Saint Catherine Labouré at Rue du Bac, Paris. As Catherine watched, Mary appeared in a frame that seemed to rotate, showing a circle of twelve stars, a large letter M surmounted by a cross, and the stylized Sacred Heart of Jesus crowned with thorns and Immaculate Heart of Mary pierced with a sword. Asked why some of her rings did not shed light, Mary reportedly replied, "Those are the graces for which people forget to ask." Catherine then heard Mary ask her to take these images to her father confessor, telling him that they should be put on medallions. Mary said, "All who wear it will receive great graces; they should wear it around the neck. Graces will abound for persons who wear it with confidence."

Initially the image was called the Medal of Immaculate Conception, but so many miracles and conversions have been worked through it that it is now simply called the Miraculous Medal. By 1842, over 100 million medals had been distributed around the world. The medal is a visible sign of the inner devotion the wearer has for Mary and her Son, Jesus.

"You, kneeling at the feet of the Immaculate Queen, must be willing not to rest until you see her reign supreme over everything and everyone, first in yourselves, then around you, in families, classes and social groups and in all private and public activities." Pope Pius XII, (September 7, 1954).

What If You Are a Non-Catholic?

First off, Catholics do not "worship" Mary. They revere her as a sublime creature of God that as the mother of Jesus she has the same influence on him in Heaven as she demonstrated at the Wedding Feast at Cana. At his crucifixion Jesus gave Mary to St. John, and St. John to his mother. At that moment Mary's role expanded to a spiritual mother for all humanity not just Catholics. Many famous saints throughout the ages have testified to her power as an intercessor with God and a great protector against evil spirits including the Devil himself.

Although a non-Catholic is unable to access the sacraments of the Catholic Church including Confession and the Holy Eucharist, nothing prevents them from following the major action steps she has given to all her children as a spiritual mother. First, as she told all the recipients of her messages at the apparition sites, "Pray, pray often to God for his mercy and protection." Holy Scripture tells us, "Ask and it will be given to you; seek and you will find;

knock and the door will be opened to you. For everyone who asks receives; the one who seeks finds; and to the one who knocks, the door will be opened" (Matthew 7:7-8). Because Jesus has given us his Blessed Mother as the great spiritual mother for all of us, we can pray to her as a heavenly advocate who intercedes for us. Everybody can pray to her and she listens.

Everyone can offer up sacrifices that have a positive ripple effect on others. Mary our mother warns us that many of our brothers and sisters are headed for damnation. We pray and trust in God to wake them up to their sinful state and change their lives to become faithful followers of God's word. We can use our suffering as a sacrifice on their behalf and for the poor souls in purgatory.

A person does not have to be devoted to Mary to pray for her guidance, protection, and intercession. She is a spiritual mother to all of us.

When we revisit all of the messages Mary has given concerning what we can do to keep Satan from carrying out destruction of the family, the Church and the world, we must first of all get our own house in order. We have our own problems with sin that offends God and hurts him deeply. Confession of our sins and sorrow for them is a crucial first step toward repentance and forgiveness. The whole purpose of the process is to provide healing for the soul and regain the grace of God that has been lost by sin.

A confession of sins relies first on something called an examination of conscience that brings the specific sins to our conscious awareness. There are various lists people can rely on to develop a working slate of one's sins. It can include the Ten Commandments, the Beatitudes, the Seven Capital or Deadly Sins or detailed lists on the Internet that serve as a reference and the basis for questions you are to ask yourself. The questions are typically connected to each commandment or capital sin. Some examples include: *Did I steal or damage another's property? Did I take the name of God in vain? Did I willfully look at indecent pictures or watch immoral movies?* Some questionnaires are designed for a targeted audience such as seniors or teenagers. I have chosen to shy away from the word "examination" and instead, prefer "illumination". The problem is that some old sinful thoughts and actions can lie hidden below our conscious mind for various psychological reasons that can still cause mental, emotional, and spiritual pain or discomfort. That brings us to the value of the "spiritual microchip" inside of us, an idea I've shared in previous books. It's a good thing.

Picture within your soul the idea of a spiritual microchip that, among other things, registers the soul's overall state of health or well-being. It can reveal the effects of sin on your soul, the good and bad things you have done to others and what others have done to you. Because it is incorporeal, scientists cannot locate it in a human body. It contains historical data that is fed to it and maintained in a spiritual memories' safety lock box.

Spiritual microchips are closely connected to something called a "life review experience" (LRE) that reportedly occurs in near-death situations when the person sees something like a video of their life played at rapid speed. People who experience it claim the phenomenon is like having their life "flash before their eyes." The individual sees an autobiographical memory playback of the history surrounding temptations unique to them. They report that the experience is so self-alarming that they greatly change their view of life and do their best to live a virtuous life from then on. The key insight they share is they see how their sinful behavior affected other people as viewed through the other person's eyes. They could feel what that person felt and see what that person saw. As one person shared: "I could individually go into each person and I could feel the pain that they had in their life... I was allowed to see that part of them and feel for myself what they felt."

In most testimonies, people who experience the life review experience phenomenon state they no longer fear death.

A spiritual microchip also is somewhat like a blackboard. As a little kid in class, I found it soothing and at times mesmerizing watching the teacher use a felt eraser to clean off the blackboard. I was happy whenever I was privileged to erase the board all by myself and watch the writing magically disappear. Then there were times when the eraser was not good enough to make the board clean. It took a big dose of water to make it clean.

I picture sins like the writing on a blackboard. Confession erases and washes away sin just like the writing on the board. It disappears, it vanishes. Thank goodness because the Devil wants us to dwell on our past sins. Why is confessing our sins so powerful in dealing with the Devil's plan of attack? First, because that is what God has promised it does. Exorcists and people who teach Catholic priests about exorcisms like Adam Blai claims, "Confessed sins are either hidden from the knowledge of the demons or not legally allowed in discourse" during an exorcism.

The Warning as described by the four visionaries at Garabandal will be a stupendous supernatural event when every person in the world will see into their immortal soul as God sees it. It will be like an illumination of conscience that can serve as a monumental "wake-up call" that will make each person face their sinfulness and decide what to do about it. Hopefully, most will cry out for mercy, repent of their sins, and change their lives for the better. As Mary told the four visionaries at Garabandal, their primary challenge is to lead "good lives". Our spiritual microchip provides an illumination of conscience that can help us do just that.

Catholics believe in something called the principal judgment an event that occurs immediately after the person dies. They believe it is too late then to change their fate as something like the life review experience passes before their eyes. "Each of us must come to the evening of life. Each of us must enter on eternity. Each of us must come to that quiet, awful time, when we will appear before the Lord of the vineyard, and answer for the deeds done in the body, whether they be good or bad" (John Henry Neuman). However, the Warning unlike the principal judgment provides an opportunity to change one's fate.

The great advantage you have is you can access your spiritual microchip and use it to start "cleaning up your act" now. When the Warning comes, I'm hoping you and I will not be as shocked and horrified to face our personal judgment at that time. Here are some helpful suggestions on how you can begin to tap into your spiritual microchip.

- First things first. Devils do not want you to use the spiritual microchip to learn how to overcome temptations and erase sins. To block their attempts, start with prayers that are specifically designed to ward off evil spirits. Use at least these three familiar prayers: The Sign of the Cross, the Lord's Prayer, and the Prayer to St. Michael the Archangel. The Saint Michael prayer is available in the appendices for you to use to cower evil spirits.

- Next, you will need to find ways of bringing your mind at ease or at peace by reining in all the scattered thoughts in a busy mind. Focus on the best times for your mind to be seemingly in neutral or very calm and relaxed. Some people find their mind to be open when they are in a shower or when they first begin to wake up in the morning before putting their feet on the floor and thinking about planning the day. For other people, it can be during the morning prayer routine when they are not feeling the pressure of time or thinking yet about their morning coffee. It might be that quiet time before going to bed before or after thinking about that day's happenings or what is coming tomorrow. If you have a little chapel or designated prayer space in your home, go there to meditate or be mindful.

- Go to the quiet place where you can pray and be open to spiritual guidance or inspiration. If you practice meditation make sure it is directly focused on Heaven above. Pray to Jesus, Mary or your guardian angel or favorite saint as you usually do to help you access your spiritual microchip. You might say, "Help me to open the treasury of the spiritual microchip so I can learn everything I need to know for overcoming temptation." Then ask them to help you to focus first on the biggest and most frequent temptation you are dealing with. "Guide me to it, open it for my enlightenment and guard me against all attempts by evil spirits to stop me."

- You want to be selective, non-judgmental, and fully open to the wisdom from the memories you will receive from the spiritual microchip. Ask for help to "get through" the embarrassing, hurtful and disgusting aspects of your behavior you could see, recall, and possibly re-experience.

- Then, go back as far as you can to first sin you remember, what prompted it and how your conscience feels about it now. Ask God to forgive you and relax allowing your mind to rest. Then allow the next sin or temptation to come into your mind and proceed with the same process. It is possible that you might receive a prompt that you need to do something about what you did back then. If so, relax and see if some type of restitution or penance comes to mind. Feel sorrow for what you did and ask God to forgive you. Complete any restitution and penance that has been brought to your mind.

- "Confession is good for the soul." Catholics confess to a priest as a representative of God and on behalf of the Church community. A non-Catholic for spiritual healing might consider asking a close friend or mate to share sins with that they trust very much and who in turn, might be willing and open to share their sins with you. You do run the risk the person might break a secret trust whereas a priest is sworn to secrecy by a sacramental seal that is inviolable. "...It is a crime for a confessor in any way to betray a penitent by word or in any other manner or for any reason" (Canon 983.1 of the Code of Canon

Law). A priest, therefore, cannot break the seal to even save his own life.

Always remember the reason for visiting your spiritual microchip is to strengthen your resistance or defense against a specific recurring temptation. You are seeking guidance on ways to fend off that temptation. Approach the adventure with optimism, an open-minded self-acceptance of who you really are in God's eyes and a heightened energy to combat the evil influences in your life. The bottom line is you want to lift off or remove the burden of sin from your life. The spiritual microchip can be a great help in overcoming sinful temptations and staying out of the Devil's clutches. "Better shun the bait, than struggle in the snare" – John Dryden

Let whatever happens to happen. Don't push, don't force, don't try too hard to make it happen. If you feel impatient or think "This isn't going to work" ask the person you are praying to for help. You may get the sense that this is not the right time or you're not ready yet for revelations. Chances are good that you will soon get a prompt to try again.

Your spiritual microchip, more than an examination of conscience, will share the good things about you as you seek to live a virtuous life. A genuine confession not only lifts a heavy burden off you, it ensures your sin is no longer on the blackboard for demons to see and work on.

Jesus told Saint Faustina that no one needs to be afraid to approach his mercy no matter how extensive or grave their sins might be, "Let no soul fear to draw near to me, even though its sins be as scarlet," because "My mercy is greater than your sins and those of the entire world." (Diary, 1485).

Epilogue

"Mary, Our Mother, sustain us in moments of darkness, difficulty and apparent defeat"- Pope Francis

In the Old Testament, God had this to say to his people at that time.

"And now, tell this to the people of Judah and the inhabitants of Jerusalem: Thus says the Lord: Look, I am fashioning evil against you and making a plan. Return, all of you, from your evil way; reform your ways and your deeds" (Jeremiah 18:11).

Mary has made it perfectly clear in her messages at Civitavecchia, Akita, Garabandal and Fatima our "ways" and our "deeds" in our modern world greatly offend God. As our mother, she appears to be at her wits' end trying to get across to us that if we do not change our ways, something bad, something we definitely deserve, is going to happen to us. It could be the Warning, the Chastisement, or a nuclear World War III. Based on the description of each of these horrendous events, the Warning poses, thank God, the least amount of devastation and loss of lives. Depending on one's viewpoint, the Warning as described by the four visionaries at Garabandal offers a hopeful wake-up call for us as Jeremiah put it, to lead people to seriously reform their "ways" and their "deeds". If enough people in our world today, unlike the time of Sodom and Gomorrah when Abraham could not come up with even ten virtuous men to save the towns from extinction), turn their lives away from sin and live out God's message through his Mother Mary, we have nothing to fear.

Once again, "If my people, who are called by my name, will humble themselves and pray and seek my face and turn from their wicked ways, then I will hear from heaven, and I will forgive their sin and will heal their land" (2 Corinthians 7:14). But we must do our part. It all starts with you and me if we want to change the world for the better and a world that's under God's love and protection. We have nothing to fear if we ask God to be near. Remember "Be not afraid, I go before you always, Come follow me…" (John Michael Talbot).

In the 1990's WWJD was all the rage. The acronyms stood for "What Would Jesus Do" prompting a question to be answered. About that time another acronym appeared known as WDJD.

It stood for What Did Jesus Do that leads to some definite answers whereas WWJD allows more speculation. Let us start with what Jesus did in the Garden of Gethsemane. The first thing he did was to ask his disciples to pray with him as he prayed fervently to his Father in Heaven. That's what we need to do. As Mary repeated over and over again, "Pray, pray, pray…pray the Rosary daily" <u>with meaning</u>. Jesus suffered greatly that night in the garden. Luke tells us he suffered so much he sweat blood through the pores of his skin.

Mary told the little children at Fatima, as did the Angel of Peace who visited them a year before, to offer up suffering and to make other sacrifices to help sinners repent in order to save them from eternal damnation. They indeed prayed as hard as they could and offered many sacrifices to help save people's souls. They did what God keeps trying to teach us repeatedly to do: love one another. What better way than to have the ripple effect of our prayers and sacrifices touch and hopefully change sinners' hearts and souls.

"Mary allowed God to take possession of her life by her purity, her humility and her faithful love. Let us seek to grow, under the guidance of our Heavenly Mother, in these three important attitudes of the soul that light the heart of God and enable Him to unite himself with us"- Mother Teresa (Letter, 1992).

Mary asks us to draw close to her to learn from her guidance how to lead purer lives, replace pride with humility and how to faithfully love God back for all the blessings He gives us and simply because God **is** love. Some people have drawn closer to Mary by wearing the Miraculous Medal. We are encouraged to consecrate ourselves and our families to the Immaculate Heart of Mary.

As it is said, "the buck stops somewhere" and in our case it is with us. Pogo said in a clever old comic strip, "We have met the enemy and it is Us." We need to clean up our act. How? First get in touch with our "spiritual microchip" (an "illumination of conscience" method) to bring to the conscious surface all the sins that have not been spiritually dealt with. Through confession, feeling genuine sorrow for having committed them, by begging for forgiveness from God coupled with a "firm purpose of amendment" (that often may require restitution and/or some other penance) we can achieve spiritual healing. In short, we need to do our part first.

Catholics have the advantage of partaking of the Sacrament of Confession, called sometimes the Sacrament of Reconciliation, and the Holy Eucharist to help them fight against all the evil temptations promoted by and thrown at them by the Devil and his demon followers. But both Catholics and non-Catholics have great prayers to help us to ward off evil spirits including the Hail Mary, the Lord's

Prayer/the Our Father and the prayer to St. Michael the Archangel for specific protection from Satan.

If we do what Mary told the visionaries at Civitavecchia, Akita, Garabandal and Fatima, as has been spelled out in this book, you and I will be prepared for any Warning or Chastisement that might come. You will be prepared knowing first of all that Almighty God created us, loves us, and wants us to follow His will for us to live "good lives". Like any good father, he sometimes must resort to shaking up the people he has created because he wants them to enjoy love, peace, and harmony in their lives. But he also gave us the gift of free will. Our fate will always remain in our control.

So, if you accept and carryout the solutions presented in the book on how to prepare for not only the great Warning, the Chastisement or for that matter, the principal judgment that comes after our death, take the following to heart:

"You will not fear the terror of night,
nor the arrow that flies by day,

140

nor the pestilence that stalks in the darkness,

nor the plague that destroys at midday.

A thousand may fall at your side,

ten thousand at your right hand,

but it will not come near you." Psalm 91:5-7

God love you. Please don't ever forget your Mother in Heaven who loves you so much and is always available to intercede for you and to protect you from all evil and who prays "for us sinners now and at the hour of our death". Amen

Saint Michael Prayer

"Saint Michael, the Archangel, defend us in battle;

be our protection against the wickedness and snares of the devil.

May God rebuke him, we humbly pray, and do thou, O prince of the heavenly host,

by the power of God, thrust into Hell, Satan and all the other evil spirits,

who prowl throughout the world, seeking the ruin of souls. Amen."

Bibliography

Primary Sources:

Daily Compass

"Civitavecchia, 'Our Lady really appeared'"

- Interview/Father Ubodi

- Costanza Signorelli, February 18, 2020

Daily Compass

"From Fatima to Civitavecchia, we are living in the Third Secret"

- Interview/Father Ubodi

- Ermes Dovico, May 16, 2020

Lifesite News

"Archbishop Viganò: Our Lady warned of 'great apostasy' in Church followed by risk of World War III'"

- Interview/Archbishop Carlo Maria Vigano

- Dr. Maike Hickson, June 2, 2020

Altervista

Interview with Jessica Gregori

- https://medjugorje.altervista.org/.../jessica.html

Interview with Fabio Gregori

- Riccardo Caniato

- http://ares.mi.it/primo-la-profezia-di-civitavecchia-911.html

Other References:

"Apostasy and loss of faith: the key is Civitavecchia"

https://ilbenevincera.wordpress.com/2015/12/31/apostasia-e-perdita-della-fede-la-chiave-e-civi

Bohlen, Celestine. "Civitavecchia Journal; Crying Madonna, Blood And Many, Many Tests", *New York Times*, April 8, 1995.

"Conchita and Loli Speak on the Aviso," Garabandal Journal, January-February 2004, p. 5. [33] Garabandal International Magazine, October-December, 2014, http://www.garabandal.org.uk/

Court Finds No Deceit With Weeping Statue "Virgin of Civitavecchia" Continues to Draw Visitors", *Zenit.org*, Zenit Staff, March 20, 2001.

"Full Text of the Third Secret Revealed". *Catholic Catholic.org*. CWR Staff, October 11, 2001.

Garabandal: The Village Speaks, Ramon Perez translated from the French by Matthews, Annette I. Curot, The Workers of Our Lady of Mount Carmel, 1985.

Hoebich, Connie. "The Warning", *Needles,* Spring 1974. https://www.garabandal.us/prph_warn

Interview with Jacinta conducted by Barry Hanratty April 16,1983, St. Michael's Garabandal Center for Our Lady of Carmel, Inc., accessed July 4, 2019, http://www.garabandal.org/News/

Kowalska, Maria Faustina. *Diary: Divine Mercy in My Soul.* Marian Press; 3rd edition, 2005.

"Our Lady of Akita", catholictradition.org/Mary/akita.htm

Pascual, Sanchez-Ventura, Francisco. *The Apparitions of Garabandal (nineteenth edition),* St. Michael's Garabandal Center, Pasadena, California, May 2019.

Petrosillo, Orazio. "'The opening' of Ratzinger: Papa Wojtyla Venerated the Madonna of Civitavecchia", *Il Messagero*, June 1, 2005.

"Sermon 2. Preparation for the Judgment", February 20, 1948, Works of John Henry Newman, Newman Reader.org. by The National Institute for Newman Studies, 2007.

St. Michael's Garabandal Center for Our Lady of Carmel, Inc. http://garabandal.org/

Sullivan, Randall. *The Miracle Detective,* Grove Press, New York, 2004.

The New American Bible, Revised Edition (NABRE). World Bible Publishing, March 9, 2011.

Timmerman, William. *Spiritual Microchips: How to Access Yours!*, Pen Shop Publishing, 2019.

Timmerman, William. *The Scary Warning from Garabandal,* Pen Shop Publishing, 2019.

Warner, Marina. "Blood and Tears", *The New Yorker*, page 63, April 8, 1996.

Watkins, Christine. *The Warning: Testimonies and Prophecies of the Illumination of Conscience.* Queen of Peace Media. Kindle Edition.

Printed in Great Britain
by Amazon

57521392R00092